A Guide to North American Waterfowl

A Guide to North American Waterfowl

Paul A. Johnsgard

 INDIANA UNIVERSITY PRESS
BLOOMINGTON · LONDON

Manufactured in the United States of America

Library of Congress Cataloging in Publication Data
Johnsgard, Paul A.
    A guide to North American waterfowl.
    "A shortened version of . . . Waterfowl of North
America."
    Bibliography: p.
    Includes index.
    1. Waterfowl—North America.   2. Birds—North
America.   I. Johnsgard, Paul A. Waterfowl of North
America. II. Title.
QL696.A5J59   598.4'1'097   78-20612
ISBN 0-253-12789-0 1 2 3 4 5 83 82 81 80 79

To J. Frank Cassel,
who taught me the difference
between seeing birds
and watching them

Contents

Plates

Trumpeter Swan
Lesser Snow Goose (Blue Phase)
Lesser Canada Goose
Atlantic Brant
Barnacle Goose
Wood Duck
American Wigeon
Gadwall
Green-winged Teal
Mexican Mallard
Florida Mallard
Northern Pintail
Blue-winged Teal
Cinnamon Teal
Northern Shoveler

Canvasback
Redhead
Ring-necked Duck
Greater Scaup
King Eider
Steller Eider
Oldsquaw
Harlequin Duck
Surf Scoter
Bufflehead
Barrow Goldeneye
Common Goldeneye
Hooded Merganser
Red-breasted Merganser
Common Merganser
Ruddy Duck

Preface

The decision to write a shortened version of my *Waterfowl of North America* was based on the fact that the majority of waterfowl enthusiasts have no real need for the detailed monographic treatment provided by a work of that size, but nonetheless are interested in learning more about each species than simply how to identify it. The lack of a book providing such a middle-ground approach to North American waterfowl encouraged me to produce one. Much of the material, such as the descriptions of ranges, subspecies, and identification criteria, was taken from the larger book with little or no modification, depending upon whether new information has become available since the publication of the earlier book. Likewise, the distribution maps are derived directly from that source. A considerable number of new drawings have been made for this book, however, and the "Natural History" sections for all species known to breed in North America have been newly written. As in the earlier book, descriptions of the natural history and biology of species not proven to breed in North America are excluded, and additionally two species limited to Mexico or the West Indies (the muscovy duck and the Cuban whistling duck) have also been eliminated from this book.

The purpose of this book is thus to allow for field or in-hand identification of North American waterfowl, and additionally to provide sufficient information on the ecology, behavior, breeding biology, and status of each species to satisfy the curiosity of most readers. A limited number of references are provided for supplementary reading.

A Guide to North American Waterfowl

The Biology of Waterfowl

The term *waterfowl*, at least as it is applied in North America, is generally restricted to the ducks, geese, and swans of the bird family Anatidae. About 140 species of this group of swimming and diving birds have survived throughout the world to the present day, and four more have become extinct during historical times. Many more species have existed in the past; the fossil record of this family extends back roughly fifty million years to very early Cenozoic times, although very little is known of the actual appearance and structure of the earliest form of waterfowl. Presumably these ancestral birds were semiaquatic, perhaps much like the modern-day species of screamers (Anhimidae), which together with the true waterfowl make up the order Anseriformes. These in turn seem to have been derived from land-adapted and fowl-like birds that later diversified into such groups as pheasants, quails, partridges, turkeys, and other "gallinaceous" species.

In part because of their common evolutionary ancestry, waterfowl and the upland, or gallinaceous, birds have certain similarities in their biology that are more fundamental than the obvious differences in their adaptations to aquatic versus terrestrial habitats. One of the most significant of these common attributes is the rather advanced, or precocial, state in which the young are invariably hatched. This implies that they are well covered with down and thus can better maintain a steady body temperature than can birds hatched naked or nearly so. They also are hatched with their eyes open, and they are sufficiently coordinated so that they can begin feeding on their own in a day or less of leaving the egg. They have a variety of calls and can respond quickly and effectively to calls of their parents that may help to keep the family together and safe from danger. They typically remain together as a cohesive "brood" during the period between hatching and initial flight, or fledging, and during this time they undergo the socialization processes that may be important later in pair formation at the time of sexual maturity. They also learn the local topography and, especially in the case of females, the landmarks necessary to allow the birds to "home" to their natal area at the time of initial nesting.

Unlike most upland game birds, nearly all North American waterfowl are migratory to some degree, and although the timing and general compass-direction tendencies for movement may be innately transmitted from generation to generation, a considerable part of the specific aspects of migration is dependent on a transmission of migratory "traditions" from the older birds to the younger ones by direct experience. This flexibility in migratory behavior accounts for the surprisingly rapid shifts in migratory pathways and stopover points that waterfowl are able to make when major environmental changes occur, such as the establishment of bird refuges, the filling of impoundments, and the like. On the other hand, this adaptability also may cause an area to be "burned out" of its waterfowl use, when disturbance or excessive mortality disrupts the traditional use of an area. This capability for human manipulation of usage by waterfowl in their migratory or wintering areas poses enormous problems for wildlife biologists, who must choose carefully between the desirability of providing safe and attractive areas for use by large numbers of birds and the potential dangers imposed by such congregations: disease or parasite transmission, crop depredations on nearby private lands, and the encouragement of unrestricted or uncontrolled hunting in areas adjacent to the controlled-usage areas. Interstate and international politics may even become involved, in view of the great economic significance of waterfowl hunting in certain parts of North America.

Usually during their first fall or winter of life, but in the case of swans, geese, and sea ducks in their second winter, the family bonds that promoted the brood's survival and transmission of migratory traditions are broken and are replaced by pair-bonding processes. The strength and duration of pair bonds in waterfowl differ greatly among species and are in general linked to the relative importance of the presence of the male in protecting the female, her eggs, or their offspring during their most vulnerable periods. Swans and geese exhibit a combination of the strongest pair bonds, the smallest clutch sizes, the longest periods of prefledging vulnerability of the young, and the longest deferral of sexual maturity. All of these interrelated characteristics suggest that the gambles associated with reproduction are much greater in these species than in the typical ducks, where conditions variably approach the opposite extreme.

Swans and geese are so large and generally so conspicuous that their nests may be readily apparent to predators, their incubation periods and fledging periods are so long that renesting attempts in the typically abbreviated nesting seasons of northern latitudes are fruitless, and the requirements for space and food adequate to rear a brood are so great that territorial behavior may limit the density and success of nesting birds in the best habitat. Thus, in keeping with the royalty often ascribed to swans, their social behavior is based on a nonegalitarian doctrine of differential social status and reduced probabilities of successful reproduction in an environment of limited resources and difficult survival.

In contrast, duck species such as mallards and other common "dabbling ducks" represent the ultimate in trends toward a democratic society. Sexual maturity follows hard on the attainment of fledging, and male mallards may begin pair-forming behavior within six months of their hatching. Pair bonds, even after they are formed, are relatively weak, and shifting about of mates may occur even without the needs generated by the death of one member of a pair. The territorial behavior by males of most duck species is weak or may even be lacking, apart from a defense of the female herself, and even this terminates shortly after the female has begun to incubate her clutch of eggs. In most ducks, the males never even see their own offspring, for by the time of hatching they have begun their vulnerable flightless period associated with the postnuptial molt. This molt may be undertaken at a considerable distance from the nesting area, the male undertaking a "molt migration" as soon as he deserts his mate. Should the female in the interim suffer the loss of her clutch or even her brood, she may remate with any available male still in suitable reproductive condition to fertilize her second clutch of eggs, and she may thereby still at least attain her own reproductive success. Parent-offspring bonds in many ducks are rather weak, promoting the development of broods of mixed family origins or even mixed species broods.

Mixing of young of different species is also facilitated by the generally weak territorial defense of male ducks, particularly toward other species. The result is that females of two or more species may nest in close proximity, or one may even inadvertently "drop" one or more of her eggs in another's nest. Nests that are used by two or more females are called "dump nests," and because of frequent fighting over nest possession the eggs are often only ineffectively incubated or not incubated at all. Such dump-nesting is most prevalent in hole-nesting species where suitable nest cavities are limited, and in such species (such as goldeneyes) true territorial behavior involving the defense of the nesting area is well developed, which would help to reduce the occurrence of mixed clutches.

Certain species of duck are much more prone to dropping their eggs in the nest of other females; this is especially true of ruddy ducks and redheads. Both species are in fact best regarded as incipient nest "parasites," since perhaps as many or more eggs are laid in other nests of their own or other species as are incubated by the females themselves. Studies to date have suggested that the hatching success of parasitically laid eggs is rather low, and virtually none of the adaptations of the highly specialized socially parasitic species of birds are to be found in these ducks. Indeed, only a single species of duck, the South American black-headed duck, is believed to be an obligate nesting parasite, since no nest of this species has yet been found. However, female black-headed ducks have been observed with flightless young, so that some doubt as to this species' total dependence on parasitic nesting still remains.

It is characteristic of all species of waterfowl to delay the start of incubation until the last egg has been laid. The length of time needed to complete a clutch varies greatly and depends on the total clutch size and the time interval between successive eggs, which is usually one or two days. During the egg-laying period the female usually spends little time at the nest, leaving it exposed to possible predation or other losses. However, in geese and swans, the male is usually present to guard the nest. As the clutch nears completion the female progressively lines the nest with down and plucked feathers, although the amount used varies considerably in different species. Swans generally use very little down in their nests, geese and ducks tend to use more, and some arctic-nesting ducks use rather large quantities, as is the case of eiders. The tropical-nesting whistling ducks normally have no down in their nests. Usually the nesting down is dark-colored, even if the other underpart feathers are white, although some hole-nesting species do have white down.

In most species of North American waterfowl the actual clutch size is variable, although the "normal" size of initial clutches may be fairly predictable, especially in species having smaller clutches. There is less variation in clutch size among high-latitude nesters than among more tropical ones, and among ground-nesting forms versus hole-nesters. Clutches that are laid late in the breeding season also tend to be smaller than the ones started earlier, and likewise repeat clutches laid by a female who was unsuccessful in her first nesting attempt are appreciably smaller than initial ones. Since the size of the clutch is also a reflection of the female's tolerance for physiological drain, the health and general fat reserves of the particular female also tend to influence the total size of the clutch. In general, clutch size tends to be smallest in swans, slightly larger in geese, larger still in surface-nesting ducks, and largest in hole-nesting ducks. Clutches also tend to average larger in low-latitude species than high-latitude ones, perhaps because of the need for effective covering and warming of the entire clutch under cold conditions, the other demands on energy reserves associated with nesting in arctic environments, or even the shorter time available for nesting and brood-rearing under these adverse conditions.

In at least some species of whistling duck, one Australian species of swan, and a very few other species of waterfowl, the male actively participates in incubation, often sharing incubation time more or less equally with the female. Among the North American waterfowl, only in the whistling ducks does the male normally participate in this way. Male mute swans, and to some extent the other swans, may regularly tend the eggs in the absence of the female, and in at least the case of the mute swan the male may take over incubation duties should the female die. Active participation by the male in normal incubation duties may also occur among the other swans to a rather greater degree than is currently appreciated, because of the difficulty of distinguishing actual incubation of the eggs from simply guarding them.

Once incubation begins, the female usually becomes very reluctant to leave the nest, and in at least some arctic species of waterfowl she may fast for the entire incubation period. It is common among temperate-zone species of duck that the female takes early-morning and late-afternoon or evening breaks from incubation, so that she may forage for a while. At this time she may be joined by the drake, if he is still in attendance. As hatching approaches, the female sits more continuously, and a certain amount of effective communication between the female and the still unhatched eggs seems to occur. The process of the exit from the egg, called pipping, may require twenty-four hours or more, and although the last-laid egg is often the last to hatch, the entire clutch typically hatches in a remarkably synchronized fashion, often within a total time span of five or six hours. Several additional hours after hatching are required for the down to dry and to fluff properly, so that the brood are likely to remain in the nest for at least the first night of their lives. By the following morning the female generally leads her brood from the nest, sometimes never to return to it. However, a few waterfowl species do use the old nest as a place to brood their young; this is especially typical of swans and of such pochards as canvasbacks and redheads, which usually construct semifloating nests of reeds well away from land. The large, bulky nests of swans also provide a convenient substitute for land-brooding and may be used for a month or more by the family, especially at night.

Although among geese and swans the parental attachment for the young persists through the entire posthatching period and the following migration, the brood bond of female ducks toward their offspring is much weaker and more variable, presumably being dependent on hormonal controls. Generally it persists through most or nearly all of the prefledging period, which may be as little as about forty days in some surface-feeding ducks and arctic-breeders, or as much as sixty to seventy days in certain diving ducks. At varying times before the young are ready to fledge, the female typically begins her post-nuptial molt, which always includes the flight feathers. Then, like the male, she becomes flightless for a time and thus highly secretive in her behavior, for she is then very vulnerable to predation and, in addition, is usually weak from the stresses associated with molting and reproduction. The length of the flightless period seems to vary considerably among species and even for the same species in different regions, but in general it is probably no less than a month and no more than two months. Thus, females of many species have often just emerged from their flightless period when they are required to begin moving toward their winter quarters. In both sexes molting of the body feathers may thus continue well into the fall migratory period. Whereas among ducks it is typical for the male to begin molting considerably in advance of the female, in geese and swans the molting of the adults is more synchronized, and indeed the female typically molts in advance of the male, often starting shortly after the young are hatched.

The timing of the fall and winter prenuptial molt back into breeding plumage varies even more than that of the postnuptial molt. Geese and swans lack a prenuptial molt altogether, and thus they exhibit virtually no seasonal variation in appearance. Evidently all ducks have a rather extensive prenuptial molt; although it is most conspicuous among males it is also present in females and affects all the feathers except those of the wings and sometimes the tail. In one North American species, the oldsquaw, there is even a third molt and a partially new plumage occurring during the winter, involving some head feathers and the scapulars. For male ducks, the timing of the prenuptial molt and subsequent assumption of the nuptial plumage is closely tied to the timing of pair-forming behavior. Social displays may begin before the males are in "full" plumage, but typically there is a close relationship between the occurrence of courtship activity and the timing of maximum brilliance of feathers and unfeathered areas such as the bill and the legs, as well as iris coloration in some species.

The intensity and complexity of pair-forming or "courtship" displays vary greatly, being under the influence of a multitude of environmental factors. These include the need for stimulating and synchronizing the sexual rhythms of the other sex, the need for sexual and species specificity to avoid homosexual matings or matings between different species, and the ecological counterpressures favoring cryptic or nonconspicuous behavior and appearance in response to varying amounts of predation danger.

With the possible single exception of the ruddy duck, all the species included in this book are ones that form monogamous pair bonds, lasting either until incubation has begun (in the case of ducks) or indefinitely, and potentially as long as both members of the pair survive (in geese and swans). For such species, there is generally a distinction to be made between the pair-forming displays that initially forge the pair bond (which require the sexual and species specificity previously mentioned) and the pair-maintaining displays that probably serve to synchronize sexual rhythms of the pair. Lastly, displays associated specifically with the facilitation of actual mating, or copulation, are needed in all species. A promiscuous species such as the muscovy duck has no need for the first two categories of display, and thus its social displays are limited to aggressive signals used in male-to-male interactions and heterosexual displays associated directly with mating.

It is interesting to note that although aggressive and threat displays used by males toward other males are obviously functional and serve to facilitate social dominance and achieve preferential opportunities for mating among the fittest mates, there is also a surprising component of aggression in the behavior of males toward females and vice versa. The reasons for this aggressive component are still speculative but obviously include the fact that the male sex hormone testosterone is closely linked with aggressiveness among vertebrates, and additionally there is a clear relationship between the ability of a male to keep other competing males away from an available female and his subsequent chances of mating with her himself. Likewise, females must be able to repel males effectively if they are to avoid constant harassment and possible rape by the still unmated males, which are usually present in considerable excess over unmated females.

The social behavior of waterfowl, like other birds, is largely dependent on communication by visual, vocal, or tactile methods, with the elements of the communication system being "packaged" in relatively nonmistakable stereotyped behavior patterns, or "displays." The repertoire of displays of any species is usually unique when the displays are considered collectively, even though some components may be identical to those of other species. The recognition of such corresponding, or "homologous," display elements is thus the basis for comparative behavioral analysis, just as the recognition of homologous anatomical elements is the basis for comparative anatomy. Thus displays are usually given descriptive names that, if well chosen, will serve to provide a shorthand means of identification for persons familiar with the corresponding display in other species. Although the same motor pattern associated with a visual display may be nearly identical in two related species, it is apparent that plumage patterns or other morphological differences may confer specificity on the two species. Likewise, differences in the tracheal anatomy of two species, such as length, diameter, and configuration, may generate acoustical differences in calls made under the same circumstances and motivation. Additionally, tension variations in the sound-producing syringeal apparatus, as well as the volume of air that is passed through it, may produce varying sound frequencies and amplitudes, resulting in characteristic call patterns that are the functional equivalent of human languages.

Following its establishment, a pair bond is maintained and strengthened by various mutual activities by the members of a pair. Among geese and swans the repeated performance of a "triumph ceremony," which is performed after the eviction of a real or symbolic "enemy" from the vicinity of the pair, is the primary behavioral bond that holds the pair together. This is generally marked by excited calling and head-waving movements by the two birds, and often also by wing-shaking or wing-waving movements as well. Among ducks, ritualized drinking and preening movements, which may differ little if at all from those normally performed as functional "comfort activities," provide a corresponding means of providing a simple mate-recognition signal system. In certain species of ducks, and particularly in the pochards and sea ducks, the same or similar signals may serve as early stages of precopulatory behavior by the pair.

Copulation is performed in the water by all the North American species of ducks. Its occurrence may be largely limited to the time immediately preceding and during the egg-laying period (as in geese and swans), or it may be much more prolonged and begin several months before the time when actual fertilization of the female is needed. To what extent such behavior might play an important role in the strengthening or maintenance of pair bonds is uncertain at present. Likewise, the significance of the generally well-developed postcopulatory displays is still rather speculative.

Raping or attempted rapes of females by males is a surprisingly common feature of the social behavior of ducks, but it is either extremely rare or totally absent among geese and swans. It has been argued by some that the raping of females whose eggs have been lost and whose mates have already deserted might provide the functional advantage of assuring the fertility of a second clutch, but this, too, is difficult to state with certainty.

Adaptations associated with foraging and food-getting are another important phase of waterfowl behavior. It is instructive to compare the diversity of bill shape and leg placement that exists among the waterfowl group as compared with, for example, the remarkable similarity of beaks and legs among the upland game birds of North America. There can be little doubt that, by these structural modifications that influence the birds' capabilities for diving, underwater activities, and extracting various kinds of foods, the waterfowl have achieved a maximum degree of habitat exploitation with a minimum of interspecies competition for the same foods. Thus, with such closely related forms as the blue-winged teal, cinnamon teal, and northern shoveler, there exists a progressive gradient in bill structure involving length, width, and relative development of sievelike lamellae. These change the bill from a tool adapted basically to probing and picking up materials from below the surface to a surface-straining device of remarkable efficiency. Likewise, the bills of swans are primarily adapted for the tearing and consumption of submerged aquatic plants, whereas those of most geese are much more efficient at clipping or tearing terrestrial herbaceous vegetation close to the ground. Similarly the heavy mollusk-crushing bills of scoters and the larger eiders differ impressively from those of their relatives the harlequin and oldsquaw, which consume large quantities of soft-bodied crustaceans, insects, and much smaller bivalve mollusks.

In parallel with species differences in bill shapes and foraging adaptations, the habitats utilized by various species of North American waterfowl differ remarkably. Freshwater, brackish, and saltwater habitats are all utilized, standing-water and flowing-water communities are likewise used, and water areas of all depths from temporarily flooded meadows to lakes several hundred feet deep are exploited for feeding and resting. Closely related species of birds that have similar bill shapes and foraging methods often differ in the habitats utilized. Thus, brackish to more saline wintering habitats are favored by red-breasted mergansers and Barrow goldeneyes, while freshwater lakes and rivers are the primary wintering areas of their respective close relatives, the common merganser and the common goldeneye. Similarly, the common mallard and black duck are associated, respectively, with open-country marshes and forested swamps for breeding, and the greater and lesser scaups are effectively segregated by habitat preference differences in both breeding and wintering areas.

Waterfowl vary appreciably in their capabilities for ready takeoff and prolonged flight; this, too, is understandable in terms of ecological adaptations. The species that are the best divers and underwater swimmers (such as the stiff-tailed ducks and the mergansers) have sacrificed aerial agility and the ease of becoming airborne for anatomical needs associated with foraging requirements. However, in such swimming "generalists" as the surface-feeding ducks that rarely have to dive for their food, the legs are placed fairly far forward and are relatively close together. This improves their walking movements on land and increases the ease of rapid takeoff from either ground or water. On land the birds simply spring into the air, while on water a combined thrusting movement of the feet and wings downward into the water instantly propels them into the air. By comparison, in order to take flight directly the masked duck must first make a shallow dive and use the associated forward propulsion of the feet and perhaps also the wings to gain the needed momentum to leave the water. Or, as in the ruddy duck, a long pattering run over fairly open water, involving both wings and feet, is required to bring the bird to "flight speed."

Speed of flight, maximum altitudes attained, and maximum duration of flight are all associated with such aerodynamic problems as "wing-loading," the configuration of the wings, and the total weight of the bird. Such heavy-bodied birds as swans are among the most slowly flying waterfowl, averaging about 35 miles per hour on short, local flights and somewhat more on long, migratory trips. On long, migratory flights swans have been found to fly as high as 10,000 feet, presumably to avoid air turbulence associated with lower altitudes. They can cover between 250 and 700 miles in a single "leg," much of which may be done in darkness. Under these conditions a star-filled sky is much more useful than a cloudy one, since overcast conditions obscure the navigational information provided by the constellations. Surprisingly, the moon is evidently of less value than the stars for nocturnal navigation, except possibly as an aid to illuminating surface landmarks.

There is an unsurpassable beauty embodied in a flock of snow geese clamoring in the sky and beating steadily toward the distant horizon, but the logistical complexities in the navigational problems, timing, and energy balances of these migrations make these esthetic considerations secondary. After enduring and surviving the fall migration southward, a female snow goose must acquire sufficient energy reserves in the form of fat during the winter to allow the 3,000-mile return flight to the breeding grounds. The arrival at the grounds must be accurately timed to within a few days. Arriving too early will mean unnecessary fasting and waiting until the nesting grounds are free of snow; arriving too late will not allow enough time for laying, incubation, and brood-rearing in the short arctic summer. The female's physical condition must allow for the energy drainage associated with a full clutch of eggs, as well as for additional fat reserves to draw on during incubation, since the presence of egg predators may not allow the female to leave the nest to eat during the entire incubation period. The female may thus lose up to a fourth of her body weight during the incubation period, and with unusually cold weather during the incubation period she may succumb to starvation or freezing only a few days prior to the hatching of her clutch. If the young do hatch successfully, the parents must tend to them as well as regain their own needed fat reserves for the energy drains associated with molting and the fall migration. Additionally, the young must be fully fledged in less than fifty days after hatching if they are to avoid perishing in the fall freeze-up. The return migration south is marked by the additional hazards of hunting and by a transmission of the traditional migratory routes to the young geese.

In short, the sight of a migrating goose flock represents far more than a simple measure of the passing seasons; it is an unwritten testimony to dogged persistence in spite of adversity, to an inherited trust in the species' long-term design for survival in the face of individual starvation and violent death. It provides a revealing insight into the workings of natural selection in a harsh and intolerant environment; the genetic blueprint for each new generation is predicted on the reproductive successes and failures of the last. It is an example that should lift the human spirit; despite individual disasters, the geese endure. Each spring they push relentlessly northward to rendezvous with fate on a distant arctic shoreline; each fall they return with the future of their species invested in a new generation of offspring. We can ask for no greater symbol of determination despite appalling hardships than is provided by waterfowl; we should be content with no less than a maximum commitment to their continued existence.

We cannot expect to learn directly from or communicate with waterfowl; they speak separate languages, hear different voices, know other sensory worlds. They transcend our own perceptions, make mockery of our national boundaries, ignore our flyway concepts. They have their own innate maps, calendars, and compasses, each older and more remarkable than our own. We can only delight in their flying skills, marvel at their regular and precise movements across our continent, take example from their persistence in the face of repeated disaster. They are a microcosm of nature, of violent death and abundant rebirth, of untrammeled beauty and instinctive grace. We should be content to ask no more of them than that they simply exist, and we can hope for no more than that our children might know and enjoy them as we do.

SPECIES ACCOUNTS

WHISTLING DUCKS
Tribe Dendrocygnini

Whistling ducks comprise a group of nine species that are primarily of tropical and subtropical distribution. In common with the swans and true geese (which with them comprise the subfamily Anserinae), the included species have a reticulated tarsal surface pattern, lack sexual dimorphism in plumage, produce vocalizations that are similar or identical in both sexes, form relatively permanent pair bonds, and lack complex pair-forming behavior patterns. Unlike the geese and swans, whistling ducks have clear, often melodious whistling voices that are the basis for their group name. The alternative name, tree ducks, is far less appropriate, since few of the species regularly perch or nest in trees. All the species have relatively long legs and large feet that extend beyond the fairly short tail when the birds are in flight. They dive well, and some species obtain much of their food in this manner. Eight species are represented in the genus *Dendrocygna*, including both of the species included in this book. A ninth species, the African and Madagascan white-backed duck (*Thalassornis leuconotus*), is considered by the author (Johnsgard, 1978) to be an aberrant whistling duck.

FULVOUS WHISTLING DUCK
Dendrocygna bicolor (Vieillot) 1816

Other Vernacular Names: Fulvous Tree Duck, Long-legged Duck, Mexican Squealer.

Range: Ceylon, India, Madagascar, eastern Africa, northern and eastern South America, and from Central America north to the southern United States.

Subspecies: None recognized by Delacour (1954). The A.O.U. *Check-list* (1957) recognizes *D. b. helva* Wetmore and Peters as a distinct North American race breeding south to central Mexico.

IDENTIFICATION

In the Hand: Like the other species in this genus, the presence of long legs extending beyond the short tail, an entirely reticulated tarsus, and an elongated and elevated hind toe are typical. The fulvous whistling duck is the only North American species with grayish blue bill and foot coloration and extensive tawny-fulvous color on the head and underparts. The wings are entirely dark on the upper surface, lacking any white or grayish white patterning.

In the Field: The most widespread species of whistling duck in North America, fulvous whistling ducks are likely to appear almost anywhere in the southern states. On water or land, their long and usually erect necks, ducklike heads, and short-tailed appearance are distinctive. At any distance, the fulvous whistling duck appears mostly tawny brown, darker above and brighter below, with the buffy yellow flank stripe the most conspicuous field mark. In flight, the long neck and long, often dangling legs are evident, and the head is usually held at or even below the body level. In contrast to the wing coloration of the other two species of whistling ducks that might be encountered in North America, the upper wing surface is neither white nor grayish white, but is instead dark brown like the mantle. The wings are broader and more rounded than in more typical ducks, and a distinctive slower wingbeat is characteristic. A whistled *wa-chew'* or *pa-cheea* call is frequently uttered, both in flight and at rest. The fulvous whistling duck feeds in rice fields and shallow marshes and occasionally comes into cornfields as well.

NATURAL HISTORY

Habitat and Foods. In the United States, the breeding habitat of the fulvous whistling duck is perhaps most extensive in Louisiana, where the birds were first proven to be nesting in 1939, and since then they have become very common breeders in rice-growing regions of that state and of Texas. Although shallow, freshwater marshes are apparently the original habitat of fulvous whistling ducks, rice fields are preferentially utilized, especially those that are heavily infested with weeds. Southward movements during fall take most fulvous whistling ducks out of the United States and into Mexico, where they concentrate in both the Pacific and the Caribbean coastal areas. A good deal of erratic movement also seems to occur during fall and winter, with individual birds or small flocks sometimes wandering northward as far as New England and even southern Canada. Throughout the year the birds are essentially entirely vegetarians, and forage both on rice and on the seeds of aquatic or shoreline weeds and grasses. When foraging they are usually found in water of swimming depth, where they may pull down the seed heads of emergent plants to strip them, or tip-up to reach

Breeding distribution of the fulvous whistling duck in North and
Central America. Recent extralimital breeding and non-breeding
records are also indicated.

shallow submerged food sources. They may even dive and remain sub-merged for considerable periods while gathering foods.

Social Behavior. Fulvous whistling ducks are highly gregarious, and even during the breeding season they tend to remain colonial. Pair bonds are strong and are presumably permanent in this species, judging from captive birds, but no proof of this exists for wild populations. Since males no more than eight months old have been observed mating, it may be imagined that at least some pairs are formed by first-year birds, and such birds have been known to breed under captive conditions. Pair-forming behavior, like that of other *Dendrocygna* species, is so inconspicuous as to remain essentially undescribed. Although "triumph ceremonies" are lacking, collective threats by small groups (perhaps extended families) often occur and may serve to maintain pair or family bonds. Copulation occurs in water of swimming depth, and is typically preceded by mutual head-dipping movements that closely resemble normal bathing behavior. Treading is followed by a spectacular "step-dance," during which the birds tread water while remaining in place.

Reproductive Biology. Unlike the black-bellied whistling duck, this species does not prefer to nest in cavities, and instead normally nests in dense emergent vegetation that is often roofed over the nest site so as to make it nearly invisible from above. Nests in water often have a ramp of vegetation leading to the rim, and frequently the nests are situated in water from 3 to 7 feet deep. Eggs are laid at the rate of 1 per day until a complete clutch of 10 to 15 is present. Incubation is performed by both sexes, and requires 24 to 26 days. The fledging period is approximately nine weeks, and the availability of a long breeding season not only facilitates this prolonged fledging period but also frequently allows for renesting by unsuccessful breeders. Shortly after the young fledge the birds begin to leave their breeding marshes in Louisiana, and the majority are gone before the start of the fall hunting season.

Conservation and Status. This species is not a significant sporting bird in the United States, and although these birds are unwary and hence readily killed, hunting is probably an insignificant source of mortality. Pesticides associated with rice cultivation are known to be a serious cause of poisoning in some areas, and the rate of loss of eggs and young in rice fields through predation or nest destruction is sometimes also quite high.

Suggested Reading. Meanley and Meanley, 1959; McCartney, 1963.

BLACK-BELLIED WHISTLING DUCK
Dendrocygna autumnalis (Linnaeus) 1758

Other Vernacular Names: Black-bellied Tree Duck, Gray-breasted Tree
  Duck, Pichichi, Red-billed Tree Duck, Red-billed Whistling Duck.
Range: From northern Argentina northward through eastern and northern South America, Central America, Mexico, and the extreme southern United States.
North American Subspecies (recognized by Delacour, 1954): *D. a. autumnalis* (L.): Northern Black-bellied Whistling Duck. North and
  Central America south to Panama. *D. a. fulgens* Friedmann is considered by Banks (1978) to be the appropriate name for this subspecies.

IDENTIFICATION

In the Hand: Like the other whistling ducks, this species has long
legs that extend beyond the short tail, an entirely reticulated tarsus, and

an elongated and elevated hind toe. It is the only whistling duck with a red bill, pink feet, or pure white on the upper wing surface.

In the Field: Whistling ducks stand in a rather erect posture on land, where their long necks, long legs, and ducklike body are evident. In the water they swim lightly, with the tail well out of the water and the neck usually well extended. The black-bellied whistling duck is easily recognized in both situations by its red bill and the large white lateral stripe that separates the brownish back from the black underparts. In flight, the long neck and trailing legs are apparent, and the blackish underparts and underwing surface contrast strongly with the predominantly white upper wing surface. Both in flight and at rest, the birds often utter clear whistling notes, the most typical of which is a four- to seven-note call sounding like *wha-chew'-whe-whe-whew*, or *pe-che-che-ne* (Leopold, 1959). As a cavity-nesting species, it is more often seen perching in trees than is the fulvous whistling duck. Like that species, it is quite gregarious and gathers in large flocks when not breeding.

NATURAL HISTORY

Habitat and Foods. This tropical-adapted species barely ranges into the United States during the breeding season, and its nesting habitat is limited to the coastal portions of southern Texas. There the Rio Grande Valley provides suitable habitat in the form of tree thickets near water where tree hollows can be found for nesting. Farther south, in Mexico, this species occurs primarily along the tropical coastlines. Outside of the breeding season flocks often move into mangrove swamps along rivers and lagoons. Like other whistling ducks, these birds are vegetarians, feeding mostly on seeds and grain of native aquatic plants and also of planted crops such as rice, corn, and sorghum. Unlike the fulvous whistling duck, this species prefers to forage while standing in shallow water, and the birds rarely have to tip-up or dive for their food.

Social Behavior. Whistling ducks tend to be highly gregarious birds, and this species is no exception. Flocks numbering as many as 2,000 birds have been reported by some observers. Like goose flocks, these groupings are made up of pair and family units that are the stable and nuclear element in the social structure. So far as is known, all whistling ducks have permanent and potentially lifelong pair bonds that presumably are established in the first or second winter of life. Little is

●B = Extralimital Breeding Records

Breeding distribution of the black-bellied whistling duck in North and Central America. Recent extralimital breeding records in the United States are indicated.

known of pair formation, which seems to be a subtle and gradual process, without obvious associated displays. Whistling ducks lack the "triumph ceremony" that is such a characteristic and conspicuous aspect of pair formation in geese and swans, and the only social display that has been well observed is that concerned with copulation. Unlike in the fulvous whistling duck, copulation occurs in quite shallow water or even on the shore, and is preceded by movements closely resembling normal drinking behavior. Following treading, both sexes call loudly and the male raises one wing slightly, but the elaborate "step-dance" of most *Dendrocygna* species is lacking.

Reproductive Biology. As females prepare to nest, they seek out suitable sites that most often consist of tree hollows that may be some distance from water. However, the location typically has a suitable perch near the nest entrance, and herbaceous rather than shrubby cover below it, which might be related to the need for the ducklings to jump from the nest entrance to the ground below when only about a day old. The clutch of 12 to 16 eggs is laid at the rate of an egg per day, and when it is completed both members of the pair participate in incubation. Competition over suitable nest sites in areas where they are limited often results in two or more females producing large clutches in "dump nests," which often leads to nest desertion. After an incubation period of about 28 days the attractive downy young hatch, and are raised by both parents. They fledge between 8 and 9 weeks of age; this leisurely growth rate is associated with tropical species and is quite different from the growth rate of arctic ducks. Families probably remain intact through the first winter, and perhaps longer.

Conservation and Status. Very few of these birds are shot by hunters in the United States, since they are rare except in southern Texas and are not regarded as attractive targets. The species is not considered to be in any danger throughout its range, and its fate is dependent on the presence of wooded tropical swamps and similar habitats.

Suggested Reading. Bolen *et al.*, 1964.

SWANS AND TRUE GEESE
Tribe Anserini

The approximately twenty extant species of swans and true geese are, unlike the whistling ducks, primarily of temperate and arctic distribution, especially in the Northern Hemisphere. It is thus not surprising that continental North America may lay claim to at least nine breeding species, or nearly half of the known total. Additionally, sufficient records of a tenth, the barnacle goose, are known as to warrant its inclusion in the book even though there is no indication that it nests in continental North America.

Several additional Old World species of geese and swans have been reported one or more times in North America, but the likelihood of at least some of these being escapes from captivity seems so great that their inclusion seems unjustified. These species include the red-breasted goose (*Branta ruficollis*), which has been collected in California at least five times and has also been seen in recent years in Texas, Pennsylvania, and Kansas, but is not known to nest nearer than central Siberia. The bean goose (*Anser fabalis*) has been reliably reported from Alaska (Byrd et al., 1974), while the smaller pink-footed goose (*A. f. brachyrhynchus*) has been collected in Massachusetts (Bent, 1925) and seen in Delaware (*Audubon Field Notes* 8:10, 9:235). Other Old World species that have been reported, such as the lesser white-fronted goose (*Anser erythropus*) and the bar-headed goose (*Anser indicus*), appear to have represented escapes from captivity, although a specimen of the former species was recently shot in Delaware (*American Birds* 27:597).

Geese and swans are generally large waterfowl that are almost entirely vegetarian in their diets. Swans forage predominantly in water, eating surface vegetation or tipping-up to reach underwater plants, but occasionally resort to eating terrestrial plants on shorelines or even in fields. Geese, however, forage both in water and on land, with some species such as brant foraging exclusively on aquatic life while others rely largely on terrestrial herbaceous plants. In most geese the cutting edges of the upper and lower mandibles are coarsely serrated in the manner of the pinking shears, providing an effective method of clipping off vegetation close to the ground. Like whistling ducks, swans and true geese have a reticulated tarsal pattern, lack iridescent or sexually dimorphic plumage patterns, and form strong, persistent pair bonds. Indeed, the fidelity of swan and goose pairs is legendary, although in actual fact this pairing behavior falls slightly short of their supposed perfect fidelity.

Although some authorities recognize a larger number of genera and species, recent investigators have generally recommended that only two or three swan genera be recognized (*Coscoroba, Cygnus,* and perhaps *Olor*) and that the genera of typical true geese be reduced to no more than three (*Anser, Branta,* and perhaps *Nesochen*). Likewise, species limits have been enlarged in recent years, so that the Old World and New World representatives of the arctic swans are now usually considered conspecific, the "blue goose" is generally recognized to be nothing more than a color phase of the snow goose, a single species of brant goose is recognized, and although a larger number of Canada goose races have recently been designated they are clearly part of an intergrading series of population complexes.

MUTE SWAN
Cygnus olor (Gmelin) 1789

Other Vernacular Names: None in general use.

Range: Breeds through the temperate portions of Europe and western Asia, as well as eastern Siberia. Introduced and locally established in New Zealand, Australia, and North America, especially along the northeastern coast, centering on Long Island.

Subspecies: None recognized. A variant, called the "Polish swan," is known to be a color phase.

IDENTIFICATION

In the Hand: Mute swans are the only white swans that have generally reddish to orange bills with an enlarged black knob at the base (lacking in immatures), outer primaries that are not emarginate near their tips, and a somewhat pointed rather than rounded tail. The trachea, unlike those of native North American swans, does not enter the sternum.

In the Field: This large swan is usually seen in city parks, but may occasionally be seen as a feral bird under natural conditions, especially in the eastern states and provinces. The neck of the mute swan is seemingly thicker than those of the trumpeter and whistling swans, and while swimming the bird holds it gracefully curved more often than straight. Further, the wings and scapulars are raised when the birds are disturbed, rather than being compressed against the body. The orange bill and its black knob are visible at some distance. In flight, the wings produce a loud "singing" noise that is much more evident than in the native North American swans, and, additionally, mute swans rarely if ever call when in flight, as is so characteristic of the native species. A snorting threat is sometimes uttered by male mute swans, which is their apparent vocal limit.

NATURAL HISTORY

Habitat and Foods. A native of Europe and Great Britain, the mute swan is normally associated there with streams and rivers, especially those supporting heavy growths of aquatic plants. Originally released in the United States on parks and estates, mute swans gradually developed a feral population as individuals escaped or were blown into new areas during storms and hurricanes. Thus the population that now breeds along the Atlantic coast from New Hampshire to Virginia was developed, and additionally a second feral population gradually formed in northern Michigan around Grande Traverse Bay and Lake Charlevoix. Scattered breedings have occurred all the way to Vancouver Island, and potentially the mute swan could become a widespread breeding species in North America in the future. Like other swans, it feeds on aquatic plants, consuming an estimated average of 8.4 pounds of vegetation per day. Thus, it may locally be a serious competitor with wintering whistling swans or possibly even trumpeter swans, in areas where these birds concentrate in winter. During the breeding season mute swans are especially intolerant of other waterfowl and have been known to kill adult geese as well as ducks, goslings, and ducklings.

Social Behavior. Like other swans, mute swans have a proverbially strong and remarkably permanent pair bond that makes them symbolic of courtship and marriage. Disruption of pair bonds is extremely rare among wild swans, and has been estimated as occurring in only about 1 percent of breeding pairs. Unsuccessful breeders are more likely to rupture pair bonds than are successful pairs, and in cases where one member

Breeding (hatched) and wintering (shaded) distributions of the mute swan in North America. Recent extralimital breeding records by apparently feral birds are also indicated.

of the pair dies or is killed there may be a gap of two or three years before the remaining bird mates again, or it may even permanently give
up pairing. Many mute swans initially breed when three years old, many
more do so when four, and a few may not breed until they are at least
six years old. There seems to be a slight tendency for females to mature
earlier than males. Copulation occurs on the water, and is preceded by
a rather prolonged series of mutual bill-dipping and preening displays.
There is also a rather well-developed mutual postcopulatory display
present, during which both birds rise almost breast-to-breast in the
water, with their necks and heads vertically extended, then slowly settle
back on the water surface.

Breeding Biology. Mute swans build large, bulky nests of vegetation
on islands or in shallow water. They are usually well isolated and in rare
cases may be clustered in colonies, where the birds are well protected
and a concentrated food source is present. Established breeders tend
to use the same nest site in subsequent years, and maintain the same
general territories. In one study, these territories were found to average
4 to 5 acres, and are strongly defended by both sexes but primarily by
the male. Both members of the pair participate in nest construction,
and about six eggs represent a normal clutch. There is a remarkably long
35- or 36-day incubation period, and all incubation is performed by the
female. Following hatching, there is an equally prolonged fledging
period of about 18 to 20 weeks, appreciably longer than the more northerly swans. On the average, about half of the young that hatch survive
to fledging, but an additional fourth are likely to succumb before the
end of their first year. Once fledging has occurred, overhead wires pose
probably the greatest threat to the survival of swans, which potentially
may live 20 to 30 years under favorable conditions.

Conservation and Status. Although the mute swan is protected
in the United States, control of local swan populations is sometimes
necessary by means of purposeful egg destruction to keep these populations from becoming too abundant. So far as can be learned, the North
American population of mute swans is still on the increase.

Suggested Reading. Willey and Halla, 1972; Scott *et al.*, 1972.

TRUMPETER SWAN
Cygnus cygnus (Linnaeus) 1758
(*Olor buccinator* of A.O.U., 1957)

Other Vernacular Names: Wild Swan.

Range: Breeds in Iceland, Scandinavia, Russia, Central Asia, Siberia to Kamchatka, the Commander Islands, and Japan (*C. c. cygnus*); in North America, isolated breeding populations currently exist in southern Alaska, British Columbia, western Alberta, eastern Idaho, southwestern Montana, and Wyoming. Introduced and breeding at various national wildlife refuges in Oregon, Washington, Nevada, South Dakota, and elsewhere. Some movement occurs in winter, but most populations are not strongly migratory.

North American Subspecies: C. c. buccinator Richardson: Trumpeter Swan. Considered by Delacour (1954) only subspecifically distinct from *C. c. cygnus,* the Whooper Swan. Recognized by the A.O.U. (1957) as a separate species.

IDENTIFICATION

In the Hand: As noted in the whistling swan account, the dorsal surface of the sternum should be examined to be absolutely certain of species identification; the presence of a dorsal protrusion near the sternum's anterior end is the best criterion of a trumpeter swan. Further, if the bird weighs more than 20 pounds (18 if less than two years old), measures at least 50 mm. from the tip of the bill to the anterior end of the nostril, and has entirely black lores or at most a pale yellow or gray mark on the lores, it is most probably a trumpeter swan.

In the Field: In the field, the absence of definite yellow coloration on the lores and a voice that is sonorous and hornlike, often sounding like *ko-hoh,* rather than higher pitched and sounding like a barking *wow, wow-wow,* are the most reliable field marks for trumpeter swans (Banko, 1960). Except within its known limited geographic range, an unknown swan should be identified as a trumpeter only with extreme care. Hansen *et al.* (1971) stated that the nearly straight culmen profile typical of this species, as compared with a concave culmen in the whistling swan, provides a useful clue for field identification.

NATURAL HISTORY

Habitat and Foods. At one time the trumpeter swan occurred widely over the plains and forests of western and central North America, extending east at least to Michigan and perhaps almost to the Atlantic coast. With egg-collecting and hunting for skins, food, and other purposes, the trumpeter's range and numbers rapidly declined, and by 1900 it was believed to be nearly extinct. The complete protection given it soon thereafter, and the gradual repopulation of part of its original range by release on various refuges, have made the species' status fairly secure. It is still most abundant in southern Alaska and in the Rocky Mountains, where lakes and marshes that are often associated with beaver activities provide its primary nesting habitat. Beaver impoundments provide stable water levels, shallow and food-rich ponds, and security from terrestrial predators such as coyotes, and are highly favored nesting sites. On such areas aquatic plants such as pondweeds, pond lilies, water buttercups, and similar submerged or emergent plants provide the major food for adults, which normally feed by submerging their heads and long necks, and at times by tipping-up to reach deeper materials. The tubers and roots of aquatic plants are also favored, and the birds often use their feet to excavate them from the bottom.

Social Behavior. Sociality is not very apparent among trumpeter swans during most of the year, and only during winter when open water

Breeding (hatched) and wintering (shaded) distributions of the trumpeter swan in North America.

or food resources become concentrated do large numbers of these birds develop in restricted areas. Family bonds are apparently rather strong, and during this period sexually immature birds may rejoin their parents, after having been evicted from their territories during the breeding season. Pair bonds are obviously strong, although no specific information on this is available for wild birds. It is known that breeding may occur as early as the third year of life, although competition for suitable territories may prevent some potential breeders from actually nesting until they are older and more experienced.

Reproductive Biology. Trumpeter swan pairs return to their territories as soon as snow and water conditions permit, and promptly begin to build a new nest or add materials to the old nest site. Frequently a muskrat house or beaver lodge serves as a nest base, but normally a week or more may be spent in adding new materials to it. Most nest construction is done by the female, with the male frequently passing materials toward the nest from its perimeter. The clutch of about five eggs is laid on a schedule of one egg every two days, with incubation beginning as soon as the clutch has been completed. Normally only the female incubates, and 33 to 35 days are probably needed to bring the eggs to hatching. The nest is vigorously defended by the male against intruders, and few mammalian predators are large enough to counter these defenses. However, many eggs remain unhatched as a result of infertility or embryonic deaths, and there is also a high prefledging mortality, especially during the first few weeks after hatching. The young require three to four months to gain the power of flight, which in some parts of the range may scarcely occur before the first cold weather of autumn. During severe winters, starvation may be an important mortality factor in Canada.

Conservation and Status. The complete protection afforded trumpeter swans came none too early, and even today most of the original breeding range of this bird remains unoccupied. The extensive prairie marshes of the Great Plains have yet to be recolonized by trumpeter swans, but with proper management it should be possible to establish breeding trumpeters on refuges over much of this region.

Suggested Reading. Banko, 1960; Hansen *et al.*, 1971.

WHISTLING SWAN
Cygnus columbianus (Ord) 1815
(*Olor columbianus* of A.O.U., 1957)

Other Vernacular Names: Wild Swan, Whistler.

Range: Breeds in arctic parts of Russia and Siberia (*C. c. bewickii*), eastern Siberia (*C. c. jankowskii*), and in arctic North America from western Alaska across the northern parts of the Northwest Territories to Southampton Island, Nottingham Island, and the Belcher Islands. The North American population winters mostly along the Atlantic and Pacific coasts, but passes through the interior during migrations, and varying numbers overwinter in northern Utah.

North American Subspecies: C. c. columbianus (Ord.): Whistling Swan. Considered by Delacour (1954) only subspecifically distinct from *C. c. bewickii*, the Bewick swan. Recognized by the A.O.U. (1957) as a separate species.

IDENTIFICATION

In the Hand: Whistling swans can only be confused with trumpeter swans when being handled; the absence of a fleshy knob at the base of the bill readily separates them from mute swans. To be certain of identification, the upper surface of the sternum must be examined to see if a protrusion near its anterior end is present, which would indicate a trumpeter swan. If this point cannot be checked, the bird is probably a whistling swan if it weighs under 20 pounds, measures less than 50 mm. from the tip of the bill to the anterior end of the nostril, and has bright yellow or orange yellow spots on the lores.

In the Field: Unless both trumpeter and whistling swans are seen together, a size criterion is of little value in the field. Rather, the differences in their voices are perhaps the best field mark, in association with the presence or absence of yellow coloration on the lores. If the lores are completely black, the bird may be of either species, but if a prominent yellow to orange yellow mark is present, the bird is a whistling swan. Further, if the voice is sonorous and hornlike, often sounding like *ko-hoh*, it is a trumpeter, whereas the voice of the whistling swan is more like a high-pitched barking sound, *wow, wow-wow* (Banko, 1960).

NATURAL HISTORY

Habitat and Foods. The name "tundra swan" has recently been proposed as a collective vernacular name for the whistling and Bewick swans, which occupy comparable breeding habitats in the New World and Old World respectively, and which are regarded by some as representing a single species. Regardless of that problem, it is clear that grassy lowland tundra is the primary nesting habitat of the whistling swan; upland tundra and rocky tundra support few if any breeding swans. During winter, whistling swans congregate in grassy river valleys, estuaries, and bays, particularly in Chesapeake Bay, Currituck Sound, and in the Central Valley of California. In Chesapeake Bay the primary wintering habitat consists of rather shallow brackish water areas, with freshwater and marine habitats being used substantially less often. Field-feeding on dry-land situations such as in cornfields is locally common and seems to be a rather recent innovation in whistling swan behavior. Like other swans, the birds are basically adapted to harvesting succulent submerged and emergent aquatic plants, including leaves, stems, and rootstalks.

Social Behavior. Whistling swans have bred so rarely under captive conditions that we still are unsure of the normal period of reproductive maturity, but probably few if any birds breed before they are four years old. This also seems to apply to the Eurasian Bewick swan, which has been much more thoroughly studied as to the social relationships of individually marked or otherwise identified birds. Studies of these swans

Breeding (hatched) and wintering (shaded) distributions of the whistling swan in North America.

in England suggest that some tentative pair bonds may be established as early as the second winter of life, but by the following winter most of these alliances have broken up and new ones have been formed. Additionally, some young swans remain with their parents through their second or even sometimes their third winter of life, which indicates the strength of family bonding in wild swans. Among hundreds of individually recognizable Bewick swans, no known cases of "divorce" have been found, and as long as three years may be taken for bereaved swans to acquire a new mate. However, in other cases mate replacement may take less than a year to accomplish. In captivity at least, swans are very long-lived, and in one instance a captive Bewick swan is known to have nested over an approximately twenty-year period with five different mates, one of which was one of her own offspring.

Reproductive Biology. In a recent study of whistling swans nesting in western Alaska, a density of only 0.14 pairs per square kilometer was estimated, which provides some idea of the large territories and dispersed breeding distribution typical of these birds. In this study the male was found to be incubating the eggs about 15 percent of the time; previous observations of captive birds suggested that only the female normally incubated. Nevertheless, there is a substantial difference in sexual involvement in these birds, with the male being especially concerned with nest defense and with covering the eggs while the female is off the nest. Like the trumpeter swan, the normal clutch size is five eggs, and the incubation period is very similar, lasting about 30 to 32 days. Following hatching, both sexes guard the young, but the male continues to perform the majority of aggressive chasing and displaying. The fledging period of the young is still somewhat uncertain, but probably requires 60 to 75 days. As soon as the young are fledged and the adults have completed their postnuptial molt the birds begin to gather and to leave the breeding areas.

Conservation and Status. It is likely that about 100,000 adult whistling swans existed in North America in the mid-1970s, about 60 percent of which are associated with Alaskan breeding grounds. In most areas they are given complete legal protection, but in a few states "experimental" hunting has been allowed, a practice that has little or no justification on economic or ecological grounds.

Suggested Reading. Scott *et al.*, 1972.

WHITE-FRONTED GOOSE
Anser albifrons (Scopoli) 1769

Other Vernacular Names: Specklebelly Goose, Tule Goose.

Range: Circumpolar; breeding from western and northern Alaska eastward across northern Canada to Keewatin, the western coast of Greenland, and in arctic Eurasia excepting Scandinavia, Iceland, and Spitzbergen.

North American Subspecies (after Delacour, 1954):

A. *a. frontalis* Baird: Pacific White-fronted Goose. In North America, breeds in arctic Alaska from the Bering Sea coast east to northeastern Keewatin and winters in the western and southern United States and adjacent Mexico.

A. *a. gambeli* Hartlaub: Gambel White-fronted Goose. Breeding grounds uncertain, probably in the MacKenzie Basin (Elgas, 1970), with most wintering occurring on the Gulf coast. Birds wintering in central California ("Tule" white-fronted geese) have recently been proposed as a new subspecies, *elgasi* (Delacour and Ripley, 1975).

A. *a. flavirostris* Dalgety and Scott: Greenland White-fronted Goose.

Breeds on the west coast of Greenland, wintering mainly in Ireland, but occasionally reaching the eastern United States.

IDENTIFICATION

In the Hand: This brownish goose can be recognized in the hand by its yellowish to reddish bill, which lacks a black "grinning patch," and its yellow to orange feet. The distinctive white forehead and the black blotching on the undersides are completely lacking in immature birds, which are almost uniformly brown in color. Domestic grey-lag geese (*Anser anser*) might perhaps be confused with white-fronted geese, but these usually have pinkish feet and legs and are considerably larger throughout.

In the Field: Both on land or water and in the air, white-fronts are notable for their rather uniformly brownish coloration, which is relieved by their white hindquarters and, at close range, by white foreheads on the adults. Sometimes their orange legs may be seen in flight, but usually at least a few of the birds in a flock will show black spotting underneath. They are generally extremely wary birds, and often utter a cackling *lee-leek* or *lee-lee-leek!*, resembling taunting laughter, while in flight.

NATURAL HISTORY

Habitat and Foods. On the breeding grounds, white-fronted geese are primarily associated with coastal tundra habitats, frequently the edges of tundra lakes, the floodplains and mouths of arctic streams, and other grassy tundra areas. Both lowland, relatively flat, tundra areas and rolling upland tundra habitats are used, and areas that have a combination of open, grassy, and shrub-fringed habitats near streams or ponds seem to be especially desirable. The "tule" form of white-fronted goose may be more dependent on heavy brush or woody vegetation for nesting than are the other races, although the breeding distribution of this subspecies is still unsettled. White-fronted geese are essentially vegetarians, feeding in the winter on grains, the vegetative parts of various grasses, and the rootstalks of cattails or bulrushes. However, this species does not "grub" for rootstalks nearly to the degree typical of such geese as snow geese, and is much more of an upland forager. Once again, the "tule" race may be an exception to this general trend,

Breeding (hatched) and wintering (shaded) distributions of the white-fronted goose in North America.

as it seems to be closely associated with marshes having emergent vegetation and apparently does little field-foraging.

Social Behavior. Perhaps because the birds nest in a rather dispersed pattern, groupings during the nonbreeding season seem to be less large than is true of the more colonial nesting geese. The birds often do mix with Canada geese while on migration and in wintering areas, and frequently feed in the same fields with them. They apparently have much the same pattern of pair-bonding and family bonding, and young birds tend to remain with their parents even through the breeding season. It has even been reported that much of the territorial defense against humans and mammalian predators is undertaken by yearling nonbreeders, which intercept intruders and attempt to lure them away from nest sites. Probably the birds normally initially nest when three years old, but under favorable conditions some two-year-olds may also attempt to nest. In a few instances, adults have been observed paired with yearlings. As in other geese, pair bonds are permanent and potentially lifelong. During the winter, much time is spent in courtship by young birds, and a good deal of aggressive behavior is evident in wintering flocks that is related to the development of social bonds.

Reproductive Biology. Upon returning to their arctic breeding areas, flocks of white-fronted geese begin to break up and to disperse widely over the tundra habitats. In a few instances nest clustering has been reported, with as many as 15 to 20 nests situated within a quarter mile. However, even on the best Alaskan tundra habitats the average breeding density is only about 6 or 7 birds per square mile. Individual females often choose low hills for nesting sites, and even in low tundra vegetation the incubating birds may be very hard to locate. The clutch size averages about five eggs, with considerable yearly variations associated with varying environmental conditions. Only the female incubates, while the male remains close at hand to help guard the nest. Incubation requires 23 to 25 days, and as soon as hatching is completed the male rejoins the family and the group moves to inland ponds, especially those providing rather heavy escape cover. The young birds fledge in a surprisingly short time, about 45 days, during which period the adults also undergo their own flightless period of about a month. The adults are thus able to fly about the same time as or shortly after the young have fledged, and leave the breeding areas soon afterwards.

Conservation and Status. Recent estimates of the late-summer populations of white-fronted geese in North America include about

250,000 in Alaska, about 50,000 in the western and central Canadian arctic, and rather small numbers elsewhere in the Canadian arctic. The actual numbers of the elusive "tule" race of the white-fronted goose are still uncertain, but wintering-grounds estimates indicate that no more than 1,000 to 2,000 birds may exist. If so, this is one of the truly rare and endangered populations of North American geese.

Suggested Reading. Mickelson, 1975; Barry, 1966.

SNOW GOOSE
Anser caerulescens (Linnaeus) 1758
(Until 1973, regarded by the A.O.U. as *Chen caerulescens and C. hyperborea*)

Other Vernacular Names: Blue Goose, Wavy, White Brant, White Goose.

Range: Breeds in arctic Siberia, on Wrangel Island, and along the arctic coast of Alaska and Canada and adjoining islands to northwestern Greenland. In North America, winters on the Pacific coast to California, the Gulf coast, the Atlantic coast south to North Carolina, and to a limited extent in the interior along the Mississippi and Missouri rivers.

Subspecies:

A. *c. caerulescens* (L.): Lesser Snow (Blue) Goose. In North America, breeds from Alaska east to Baffin Island and winters primarily in the central valley of California, the Gulf coast, and in the Mississippi Valley north to Missouri.

A. *c. atlanticus* (Kennard): Greater Snow Goose. Breeds in north-western Greenland and on Baffin, Devon, and probably Grinnell islands and winters along the middle Atlantic coast south to North Carolina.

IDENTIFICATION

In the Hand: Snow geese are likely to be confused in the hand only with Ross geese and perhaps with immature white-fronted geese. On examination of the bill, the presence of the black "grinning patch" and the absence of warty protuberances at the bill's base should indicate a snow goose, and additionally no goose with a folded wing longer than 400 mm., a culmen longer than 50 mm., and a weight of more than 4 pounds (or 2,000 grams) would be a Ross goose. Young blue-phase snow geese sometimes are confused with young white-fronted geese, but the yellowish legs, feet, and bill and the lack of a black grinning patch will serve to distinguish young white-fronted geese. Domestic white geese might be confused by hunters with snow geese; these birds lack black wingtips and have no black grinning patch.

In the Field: Both in the air and on the ground or water, snow geese are readily identified by the partially or extensively white plumage, contrasting with the dark flight feathers. Wild snow geese call almost constantly, and their rather shrill, repeated "*la-uk!*" notes are reminiscent of barking dogs. In flight the emperor goose might be confused with a blue-phase snow goose, but this dark phase does not occur in the range of the emperor goose, and additionally emperor geese exhibit dark rather than white tail coverts in flight. Snow geese usually travel in larger flocks than do white-fronted geese, and even at a considerable distance the underwing coverts of white-fronts appear nearly as dark as their primaries, while in "blue" geese the anterior underwing coverts are much lighter, and they also show much more white around the head.

NATURAL HISTORY

Habitat and Foods. Lesser snow geese prefer to nest on low, grassy tundra located near salt water, lakes, ponds, or on river floodplains. The arctic-nesting greater snow goose more typically nests where stony terrain meets wet and grassy tundra, or where low and marshy tundra is protected from the north by mountains. Both subspecies are highly

Breeding (hatched) and wintering (shaded) distributions of the snow goose (lesser snow goose horizontal hatching, greater snow goose vertical hatching) in North America.

colonial during the nesting season and extremely gregarious during the rest of the year. They thus tend to feed in areas rich in their primary foods, which are grasses, grains, sedges, and various broad-leaved herbaceous plants. In contrast to Canada geese and white-fronted geese, which often occur in the same general migratory and wintering areas, snow geese tend to be "grubbers," pulling up plants by the roots and consuming both the stalks and roots. They also crop short grasses very effectively in the usual manner of *Anser* geese. In the midwestern states the birds often feed in cornfields, where they not only are able to pick up waste grain from the ground but also can strip corn from cobs quite effectively.

Social Behavior. Although snow geese may form pair bonds in their second winter of life, they evidently are only rarely successful at breeding as two-year-olds. Pair formation thus probably occurs between the second and third winters of life, and as in other geese seems to be a rather gradual process. In the lesser snow goose, where there are two genetically determined color phases, it has been learned that mate choice is rather strongly influenced by early experience, with birds tending to pair with individuals that match the color phase of their parents. Since the phase of parent and that of offspring are usually the same, the incidence of mixed matings and thus heterozygotic or "hybrid" offspring is considerably less than would be brought about by random matings. In recent decades, however, the "blue" phase of the lesser snow goose has become relatively more common on more northerly and westerly breeding grounds, and it has been suggested that this change in gene frequency in such regions may have been caused by movements of intermediate individuals rather than by pioneering on the part of pure blue-phased birds.

Reproductive Biology. Snow geese often arrive on their breeding grounds just as the terrain is beginning to become snow-free, and older pairs initiate new territories or reestablish old ones as quickly as possible, leaving the younger and less experienced pairs to develop their territories around the periphery of the colony. The birds often nest near or among other arctic geese, such as brant or Canada geese, and also sometimes nest close to snowy owls, presumably for protection from other potential egg predators such as gulls and jaegers. The four- to five-egg clutch is laid at the rate of one egg per day, and the female begins incubation as soon as the clutch has been completed. During the 22- to 23-day incubation period the female scarcely leaves the nest, and the male remains nearby to help defend it from arctic foxes or other possible disturbances. Because of her fasting during incubation, the female loses a good deal of weight and may even freeze or starve to death on the nest if she is not in ideal physical condition at the onset of nesting. The young leave the nest only a few hours after they all have hatched, and usually are led by the parents out of the nesting colony to safer areas, such as shallow lakes or the tidal zone, for brood-rearing. They fledge in about six weeks, and soon thereafter the birds begin to flock for their southward migration.

Conservation and Status. In recent decades the greater snow geese have staged a remarkable population upsurge, and by the early 1970s had exceeded 100,000 birds. The lesser snow goose has also responded very well to management, and some of its major problems at present concern overcrowding on various migratory and wintering areas that pose serious problems in the control of infectious diseases such as fowl cholera. During the early to middle 1970s there were well over a million lesser snow geese wintering in the United States and Mexico.

Suggested Reading. Johnsgard, 1974.

ROSS GOOSE
Anser rossii Cassin 1861
(*Chen rossii* of A.O.U., 1957)

Other Vernacular Names: None in general use.

Range: Breeds mainly in the Perry River region of the Northwest Territories eastward along the Queen Maud Gulf to at least 97°02′ W. latitude, and southward in the interior to at least 66°21′ n. longitude (Ryder, 1967), and winters mostly in central California, with vagrant birds occasionally reaching the midwestern states and rarely the eastern states. Limited breeding also occurs on Banks and Southhampton islands and on the McConnell River, Keewatin District.

Subspecies: None recognized.

IDENTIFICATION

In the Hand: Although the Ross goose is normally found only within a limited winter and summer range, it occasionally strays far from its usual migratory route, and individual birds may turn up almost anywhere. If examined in the hand, Ross geese exhibit a short bill (under 47 mm.) that may be black along the edges but has no definite "grinning patch" and in adult males is usually warty near its base, which is bluish. Ross geese also never exceed 4 pounds (or 2,000 grams), and their folded wing measurements never reach 400 mm.

In the Field: Ross geese are best distinguished by direct size comparison with snow geese when they are in the same flock, or by their comparable size to large ducks, such as mallards. The bluish base of the bill may be evident at fairly close range. Some birds of intermediate size and appearance have been seen in wild flocks, indicating that natural hybridization does occur and thus adds to the difficulties of field identification of Ross geese among snow goose flocks (Trauger *et al.*, 1971).

NATURAL HISTORY

Habitat and Foods. Breeding habitat of the Ross goose is much like that of the snow goose, but to a considerably larger degree the Ross goose is dependent on islands in lakes for nesting. These islands provide, in the form of rocks and shrubs, physical protection from wind and to some extent from rain and snow, but more importantly they provide protection from predation by arctic foxes. Ideal lakes are thus those that are large enough that predators cannot swim across to the islands, but shallow enough that ice bridges are not present at the start of the nesting season. Additionally, the availability of food in the form of grasses and sedges is of major importance in determining the location of nesting colonies. In the nonbreeding season Ross geese often mingle with and share habitats with the lesser snow geese in western states, and probably feed on identical foods. Their shorter bill presumably allows the Ross geese to crop shorter grasses, and like the lesser snow goose they sometimes also grub for roots. In the fall they are often found in wheat and barley fields, where they feed on waste grain.

Social Behavior. Like the lesser snow goose, this species is highly colonial and gregarious. In a few areas they share nesting grounds, where they doubtless are at a disadvantage when competing for territorial space or nesting sites. In recent years, a rather surprising number of apparent hybrids between the two species have been found, which complicates the taxonomic interpretation of this already complex evolutionary problem. However, pair bonds are presumably formed on wintering areas in the second or possibly third winter of life, and most birds probably initially breed in their third year. Pair bonds, once established, are permanent, and family bonds also seem to be quite strong, since yearlings remain with their parents until incubation of the next clutch of eggs is begun. Ross geese are extremely tolerant of crowding on the nesting grounds; in areas of high concentrations territories may be as

Breeding (hatched) and wintering (shaded) distributions of the Ross goose in North America.

small as 10 feet across, and the average distance between nests is about 15 feet.

Reproductive Biology. Female Ross geese build their nests on a variety of substrates, but the preferred location is an environment of small birch stands and rocks, where ample protection from the elements and adequate space for grazing can be found. There is a surprisingly small average clutch of about four eggs, and birds that initiate their nests only a few days later than normal have even smaller clutches. It has been suggested that the small average clutch size of this species evolved in relation to average food availability and maximum energy reserves of the female. By laying a small clutch the female avoids depleting her postlaying energy reserves, and thus increases the likelihood that she can effectively incubate and brood her eggs and young. Incubation lasts about 22 days, with the male remaining close at hand; as soon as the eggs have hatched he joins the group. Thereafter, the male undertakes the defense of the family, as the female leads the brood away from any source of danger. The young birds fledge in about 40 to 45 days, and by that time the adults have completed their postnuptial molt, thus allowing the onset of the fall migration.

Conservation and Status. Although for many years the status of the Ross goose was regarded as precarious, the species has undergone a gradual and prolonged improvement in numbers, so that by the mid-1970s it was probably approaching 100,000 birds. Confusion with lesser snow geese on the wintering grounds makes accurate counting difficult, but it is certain that the Ross goose is in no present danger.

Suggested Reading. Ryder, 1967.

EMPEROR GOOSE
Anser canagicus (Sewastianov) 1802
(Philacte canagica of A.O.U., 1957)

Other Vernacular Names: Beach Goose.

Range: Breeds in coastal Alaska from the mouth of the Kuskokwim River to the north side of the Seward Peninsula, St. Lawrence Island, and on the northeastern coast of Siberia. Winters on the Aleutian Islands and along the Alaska Peninsula probably to Cook Inlet with vagrant birds wintering in British Columbia and the western United States south to California.

Subspecies: None recognized.

IDENTIFICATION

In the Hand: Emperor geese can hardly be confused with any other species when in the hand; the multicolored reddish bill lacking exposed "teeth," the yellowish legs and feet, and a scalloped feather pattern of gray, black, and white are all unique.

In the Field: Along their very limited range, emperor geese are usually found along saltwater shorelines, where they occur in small flocks. The golden to orange staining on their white head feathers is conspicuous and contrasts with the otherwise grayish plumage. In flight, the lack of white feathers above or below the tail makes this species unique among geese. They also have relatively short necks and heavy bodies, associated with a rapid and strong wingbeat. In flight, the birds often utter a repeated *kla-ha* or an alarm note *u-leegh*.

NATURAL HISTORY

Habitat and Foods. Throughout its North American range, the emperor goose prefers to nest in low, wet tundra, usually near the coast and often near lakes or ponds. Ponds or lakes surrounded by low, rolling hills and somewhat inland from tidal areas are preferred breeding habitat in Alaska, while in Siberia the birds are usually found on coastal flats, especially near the mouth of small rivers. Food habitat studies made during spring and summer indicate that this species is primarily vegetarian, living on plants associated with the tidal zone, such as algae, eelgrasses, and pondweeds, with eelgrass particularly favored. Sedges are also eaten in large quantities in spring as soon as green vegetation begins to appear, as are grasses and some animal materials. During fall and winter a larger amount of animal foods are eaten, since at that time of year the birds are mainly found around the Aleutian and Commander islands, where they often feed along the beaches in the tidal zone.

Social Behavior. Like other geese, emperor geese have strong and permanent pair bonds and relatively strong family bonds. Disintegration of the family bond apparently occurs among wintering flocks during the first winter of life, when aggression toward yearlings begins, and becomes completed by the time the birds have returned to their breeding areas. Presumably formation of pairs also occurs in wintering areas among two-year-old birds; in captivity emperor geese show essentially the same pattern of triumph ceremonial behavior and behavior associated with copulation as do the other typical geese. In the wild, copulation probably occurs just before and during spring migration, so that the females have been fertilized by the time they arrive on their breeding areas. Shortly after they arrive they begin to select nesting sites, and territorial displays become more intense. A rather small territory of about 14 square meters is defended around the nest site, with the male undertaking the

Breeding (hatched) and wintering (shaded) distributions of the
Emperor goose in North America.

major defensive role, and excluding his yearling offspring just as strongly as rival pairs are repelled.

Reproductive Biology. Emperor geese frequently select nesting sites used in previous years, and some sites may be used as many as three successive seasons. The nests are most frequently situated in vegetative growth of the previous year, and usually are in slightly elevated situations that allow for excellent visibility and good drainage. The first egg is usually laid on the same day that the nest is constructed, and thereafter eggs are laid at approximate daily intervals until the clutch, averaging five eggs, has been completed. Incubation begins with the completion of the clutch and is performed only by the female, with the male defending the site. Although females leave their nests for short periods during the early stages of incubation, they sit almost continuously during the late stages, feeding on vegetation immediately around the nests and drinking dew or water from small depressions. The average incubation period is 24 days, and the brood normally leaves the nest within 48 hours of hatching. A surprising amount of brood movement has been found in a recent Alaskan study, with broods often moving several kilometers to brood-rearing areas, and in one case probably moving nearly 20 kilometers over a period of a few days. The young birds' fledging period has not been definitely established but is probably about 50 to 60 days, and allows them to attain flight by the end of August in most cases. The birds remain in family groups through the fall migration to the wintering grounds.

Conservation and Status. Both the primary breeding grounds and the major wintering areas of this species are well removed from most human activities, and it is believed that the total world population varies from 175,000 to 200,000 in the fall to 140,000 to 160,000 in the spring. At present there is no way of determining whether the population is increasing, is stable, or is declining.

Suggested Reading. Eisenhauer and Kirkpatrick, 1977.

CANADA GOOSE
Branta canadensis (Linnaeus) 1758

Other Vernacular Names: Cackling Goose, Canadian Goose, Honker, Hutchins Goose, Richardson Goose, White-cheeked Goose.

Range: Breeds across most of North America, from the Aleutian Islands across Alaska and northern Canada and south to the central United States. Resident flocks of larger subspecies are also established at many wildlife refuges, in some cases well beyond the probable original range of the subspecies. Also introduced into New Zealand, Great Britain, and Iceland.

North American Subspecies (based on Delacour, 1954):

B. *c. canadensis* (L.): Atlantic Canada Goose. Breeds in southeastern Baffin Island, eastern Labrador west probably to the watershed line, Newfoundland, Anticosti Island, and the Magdalen Islands.

B. *c. interior* Todd: Hudson Bay (Todd) Canada Goose. Breeds in northern Quebec, Ontario, and Manitoba around Hudson and James bays, south to about 52° N. latitude and north as far as Churchill and the Hudson Strait.

B. *c. maxima* Delacour: Giant Canada Goose. Originally bred on the Great Plains, from the Dakotas south to Kansas, Minnesota south to Missouri, western Kentucky, Tennessee, and northern Arkansas. Now largely limited to planted flocks in wildlife refuges. Hanson (1965) considers the geese that breed in southern Canada from Alberta to Manitoba to represent this race.

B. *c. moffitti* Aldrich: Great Basin (Moffitt) Canada Goose. Breeds in the Great Basin of North America between the Rocky Mountains and the eastern parts of the Pacific states, intergrading to the north with *parvipes* and to the east with *interior* and probably originally also with *maxima*.

B. *c. parvipes* (Cassin): Athabaska (Lesser) Canada Goose. An intermediate and ill-defined form that links the larger, southern subspecies with the small, northern and tundra-breeding populations. Breeds from central Alaska eastward across northern Canada and southern Victoria Island to western Melville Peninsula and eastern Keewatin southward to the northern parts of the Canadian Prairie Provinces, where it intergrades with *moffitti*.

B. *c. taverneri* Delacour: Alaska (Taverner) Canada Goose. Probably breeds through much of the interior of Alaska, some distance from the coast, from the base of Alaska Peninsula to the Mackenzie River delta, intergrading locally with *minima, occidentalis*, and probably also with *parvipes*. Not recognized by the A.O.U. (1957); apparently considered part of *minima* and *parvipes*.

B. *c. fulva* Delacour: Queen Charlotte (Vancouver) Canada Goose. Breeds along the coast and islands of British Columbia and southern Alaska, north to Glacier Bay, largely nonmigratory.

B. *c. occidentalis* (Baird): Dusky (Western) Canada Goose. Breeds along the Prince William Sound, Cook Inlet, and inland through the Cooper River drainage, east to Bering Glacier.

B. *c. leucopareia* (Brandt): Aleutian Canada Goose. Rare; limited to a few of the Aleutian Islands such as Buldir; recently (1978) released on Agattu. The name *leucopareia* has also been applied earlier (e.g., Aldrich, 1946) to the populations here recognized as *parvipes* and *taverneri*.

B. c. asiatica Aldrich: Bering Canada Goose. Extinct; once bred on the Commander and the Kurile islands.

B. c. minima Ridgway: Cackling Canada Goose. Breeds along the coast of western Alaska from Nushagak Bay to the vicinity of Wainwright, where it probably intergrades with *taverneri*.

B. c. hutchinsii (Richardson): Baffin Island (Richardson) Canada Goose. Breeds on the coast of the Melville Peninsula, Southhampton Island, western Baffin Island, Ellesmere Island, and perhaps western Greenland. Intergrades with *parvipes* in Keewatin (MacInnes, 1966). Apparently extends west to Victoria Island (Parmelee *et al.*, 1967).

IDENTIFICATION

In the Hand: Even in the juvenal plumage, the distinctive dark head and neck with the lighter cheeks and throat are evident. Because of this, the Canada goose could be confused only with the barnacle goose, from which the Canada can be distinguished by the absence of white feathers over the forehead connecting the white cheek patches. (Some large Canada geese may have a small white forehead patch that is discontinuous with the cheek markings.) Canada geese also lack the definite black and white tips on the upper wing coverts typical of barnacle geese.

In the Field: Even at great distance, Canada geese are usually readily recognized by their black heads and necks, brownish body and wings, and white hindpart coloration. This combination also applies to brant geese, but these small geese are limited to coastal waters and may be recognized by their short necks and ducklike size. The small races of Canada geese also have relatively short necks, with the neck length becoming progressively greater as the body size increases, so that the largest forms of Canada geese appear to be unusually long-necked. When in flight overhead the birds show uniformly dark underwing coverts of about the same color as the primaries and, except for their black necks, might be easily mistaken for white-fronted geese if the latter's dark abdominal spotting is not visible. The smaller races have high-pitched "cackling" calls sometimes sounding like *luk-luk*, while the larger forms have "honking" notes often sounding like *ah-onk'*.

Breeding and wintering distributions of the Canada goose in North America. Approximate breeding distributions of subspecies are indicated.

NATURAL HISTORY

Habitat and Foods. Since the Canada goose has such a remarkably broad breeding range, and is subdivided into numerous subspecies having widely divergent ecological adaptations and habitat needs, it is almost impossible to present in capsule form a statement on habitat requirements. Nearly all the nonmountainous areas of continental Canada and Alaska can be considered breeding habitat, and additionally Canada geese once bred widely over the Great Plains and Great Basin of the United States. Wintering areas also range from coastal estuaries to impoundments and lakes in the continental interior, wherever there is a combination of safe roosting sites and extensive food in the form of agricultural crops or native grasses and other edible herbaceous plants. Canada geese are essentially terrestrial grazers, but also feed on many marsh plants and on grains, especially corn.

Social Behavior. Canada geese probably become reproductively active their second winter of life under normal conditions, although rarely yearling males may attempt to breed and particularly in the arctic-adapted races the most common age of initial breeding seems to be three years. Pair bonds are strong and essentially lifelong. However, separation from a mate, or its death, results in the formation of a new pair bond, usually during the next breeding season. In older, experienced, and "acquainted" geese, pair bonds can be formed very rapidly, even in a few hours, and such bonds will persist as long as both members remain alive. Apparently pairing occurs on the nesting ground when the young are two years old, although some yearlings form temporary pair bonds. However, broodmates retain family bonds well into their second year, and migrating flocks of Canada geese basically consist of units comprised of pairs and families, with no single "flock leader" as is often imagined.

Reproductive Biology. Nest-building is normally done by the female almost exclusively, although rarely the male participates to a limited extent. Nests are usually well dispersed over the available habitat, but in some situations where favored nest sites are highly limited, such as on islands or in relatively safe situations, a considerable amount of crowding may be tolerated. Generally, Canada geese prefer to nest in locations that allow good visibility, a firm and fairly dry nest foundation, close proximity to water, and nearness to suitable foraging and brood-rearing habitats. Elevated sites are preferred over lower ones, and sand seems to be preferred over cobblestone as a substrate. The eggs are laid at approximately daily intervals until a clutch averaging about five eggs has been completed. There is no obvious geographic variation in clutch sizes, but incubation periods tend to be slightly shorter (about 24 versus 28 days) in the smallest as compared to the largest subspecies. Likewise, the fledging periods of the small, arctic-adapted races are sometimes as short as 42 days, while in the largest races as long as 86 days may be required to attain flight in young birds. In all the races, the adults undergo their own flightless periods during the latter part of the fledging period of their offspring, and larger forms remain flightless for longer periods than do the smaller ones. In some races there is a substantial "molt migration" by adult nonbreeders, which may fly a thousand miles or more to traditional molting areas before becoming flightless.

Conservation and Status. As a species, the Canada goose has responded extremely well to management, and now is more common in some areas than ever before in historical times. However, a few races remain in danger, particularly the Aleutian Canada goose, whose breeding range had contracted to a single island (Buldir) until efforts were made to reestablish it on other Aleutian Islands. Efforts are continuing in this regard, and the population of the race has in recent years increased from a few hundred known birds to approximately two thousand by the late 1970s. Likewise, the "giant" Canada goose has benefited from efforts to reestablish it over much of its original prairie breeding range.

Suggested Reading. Williams, 1967.

BARNACLE GOOSE
Branta leucopsis (Bechstein) 1803

Other Vernacular Names: None in general use.
Range: Breeds in northeastern Greenland, Spitzbergen, and southern
Novaya Zemlya. Winters in Ireland, Great Britain, and northern
Europe, with only rare occurrences in eastern North America.
Subspecies: None recognized.

IDENTIFICATION

In the Hand: This small, dark-breasted goose may be identified by
its white cheeks and forehead, its black breast, and the grayish upper
wing coverts that are distinctively tipped with black and white.

In the Field: Only an occasional visitor to North America, the
barnacle goose nevertheless has appeared in a surprising number of lo-
calties, mainly along the eastern coast. It is slightly larger than a brant
and differs from it in having a predominantly white head and a light
gray rather than dark grayish brown upper wing coloration. The underwing coloration is likewise light silvery gray and much lighter than that
of the brant. The extension of the black neck color over the breast will
readily separate the barnacle goose from the Canada goose, even at a
great distance, and the contrast between the dark and light parts of the
body is much greater as well. Its call is a barking, often repeated *gnuk;*
a flock sounds something like a pack of small dogs.

BRANT GOOSE
Branta bernicla (Linnaeus) 1758

Other Vernacular Names: American Brant, Black Brant, Brent.

Range: Circumpolar, breeding along arctic coastlines of North America and Eurasia, as well as on Greenland, Iceland, and other arctic islands. Winters on coastal areas, in North America south to northwestern Mexico and North Carolina.

North American Subspecies:

B. b. *hrota* (Müller): Atlantic Brant Goose. In North America, breeds on northern and western Greenland and on the mainland coast and islands of northern Canada west to about 100° W. longitude.

B. b. *nigricans* (Lawrence): Pacific (Black) Brant Goose. In North America, breeds in northern Canada from the Perry River and adjacent islands westward to coastal Alaska. Considered by Delacour (1954) to represent B. b. *orientalis* (Tougarinov), with *nigricans* restricted to the questionably valid "Lawrence brant goose," which is not recognized by the A.O.U. (1957). The proper application of *nigricans* to any population of brant is still questionable (Manning *et al.*, 1956; Williamson *et al.*, 1966).

IDENTIFICATION

In the Hand: The tiny size (under 4 pounds, or 2,000 grams) will separate this species from all others except the smallest races of Canada geese, which have white on their cheeks instead of on the upper neck. Also, the central tail feathers of Canada geese extend beyond the tip of the tail coverts, which is not true of the brant goose.

In the Field: In their coastal habitat, brant are usually seen in small flocks on salt water some distance from shore, their white hindquarters higher out of the water than is typical of ducks. The head, neck, and breast of this bird appear black, the sides grayish to whitish. When in flight, the birds appear short-necked, and the white hindquarters contrast strongly with the black foreparts, while both the upper and lower wing surfaces appear grayish brown. The birds usually fly in undulating or irregular lines, rather than in V-formations like Canada geese, and have surprisingly soft and gutteral notes, *r-r-r-ruk* or *ruk-ruk*.

NATURAL HISTORY

Habitat and Foods. The breeding habitat of brant geese consists of lowland coastal tundra, usually close to the tide line, where slowly flowing streams cut through sedge and grass-covered flats. Rarely brant will nest as far as five miles from the coast, but typically such inland nests are well scattered, while in coastal situations the nest density may be as high as 150 nests per square mile. Food habits during the breeding season are not well studied, but the diet probably consists mostly of grasses and sedges. Outside the breeding season the birds are closely associated with the distribution of eelgrass. In areas where eelgrass is lacking, the birds consume sea lettuce and, to a lesser degree, wigeon grass. During periods when eelgrass beds have been depleted by disease, the wintering distribution of brant has been affected. At such times they may resort to foraging in meadows near the coast.

Social Behavior. Brant geese are highly social birds, and begin to form flocks shortly after the young have hatched. This results in mixed broods often tended by more than one pair of adults. Although a small proportion of brant may nest when two years old, it is believed that most birds do not successfully breed until they are three years of age. Courtship occurs on wintering areas between January and April, and presumably involves both first- and second-winter immature birds, and adults that have lost their mates. Brant have triumph ceremonies similar to those of other geese, and additionally aerial display flights involving a female and two or more males are frequent among wintering flocks. Copulation occurs on water, and the associated preceding be-

Breeding and wintering distributions of the brant goose in North America. Horizontal hatching indicates breeding range of Pacific brant, vertical hatching that of Atlantic brant, and diagonal hatching apparent area of intergradation.

havior, much like that of other geese, consists of a mutual display resembling bathing movements.

Reproductive Biology. Like other geese, brant arrive on the nesting areas as pairs, and the birds quickly begin to seek out suitable nest sites, often on small islands or peninsulas where the danger of predation by foxes is probably reduced. The birds nest in a semicolonial manner, and a substantial proportion of nests are located in sites that had been used the previous year, presumably by the same birds. Eggs are laid at the rate of one per day, and the average clutch size is usually close to four eggs. There are, however, considerable year-to-year variations in clutch size, associated with weather at the time of nest inception. Males remain very close to their mates throughout the incubation period, although the tiny size of these birds makes them rather ineffective in preventing predation by foxes or by the larger avian predators, such as glaucous gulls. These gulls and jaegers are also very serious enemies of young goslings, especially during the first week or two of life. The incubation period averages 24 days, and another 45 to 50 days are required to bring the young birds to fledging. The young birds are led away from the nest soon after hatching, usually moving to the tidal flats where they feed on larvae and small crustaceans. At this time the adults also undergo their month-long flightless period, and frequently both adults and young attain the power of flight only shortly before the onset of freezing weather.

Conservation and Status. Although there have been some very substantial fluctuations in the numbers of brant in eastern North America, as well as major changes in their wintering areas, the Pacific coast population has generally remained above 100,000 birds in recent years. The Atlantic coast population has ranged from a high of 266,000 in 1961 to less than 50,000 in the early 1970s, and these recent variations have principally been the result of varying conditions on the arctic breeding grounds. Because of its high-arctic nesting tendencies, and the fact that colonies are so strongly affected by storm tides, reproduction in some years may be almost nil.

Suggested Reading. Mickelson, 1975; Barry, 1966.

PERCHING DUCKS
Tribe Cairinini

The perching ducks and related gooselike forms are a diverse array of some fourteen species that are largely subtropical to tropical in occurrence. Although they vary in size from as little as about a half a pound in the "pygmy geese" (*Nettapus*) to more than twenty pounds in the spur-winged geese (*Plectropterus*), all possess some common features. These include a tendency toward hole-nesting, especially in trees; sharp claws; associated perching abilities; and long tails that presumably increase braking effectiveness when landing in trees. Nearly all species exhibit extensive iridescent coloration in the body, especially on the upper wing surface; this coloration is often exhibited by females as well as males. As a result, this tribe includes some of the most beautifully arrayed species of the entire family, of which the North American wood duck is an excellent example, as is the closely related Asian mandarin duck (*Aix galericulata*). The wood duck is the only perching duck that is native to the United States or Canada.

Perching ducks, together with all of the following groups of waterfowl included in this book, are representatives of the large anatid subfamily Anatinae. Unlike the whistling ducks, swans, or true geese, species of this subfamily have a tarsal scale pattern that has vertically aligned scutes (scutellate condition) above the base of the middle toe, and the sexes are usually quite different in voice, plumage, and sexual behavior. These sexual differences can be attributed to the weaker and less permanent pair bonds characteristic of true ducks, with a renewal of pair bonds typically occurring each year. As a result, pair-forming behavior tends to be more complex and elaborate in these species, as a dual reflection of the greater and more frequent competition for mates and the need for safeguards in reducing or avoiding mixed pairings between species during the rather hurried pair-forming period. In these species, the males typically assume the initiative in pair-forming activities, and thus they are usually more colorful, more aggressive, and have the more elaborate pair-forming behavior patterns. On the other hand, the females retain a subdued, often concealing plumage pattern, associated with their assumption of most or all incubation and brood-rearing responsibilities. As a result, humans usually find it easy to recognize the distinctively plumaged males of most species, while the females of related species are often so similar that even experienced observers may find it difficult to identify them with certainty.

Following the initiation of incubation, the males in this subfamily typically abandon the females and begin their postnuptial molt, during which they become flightless for a time and usually also acquire a more femalelike body plumage. Thus, unlike the species in the subfamily Anserinae, typical ducks have two plumages, and thus two body molts, per year. In males this double molt is most apparent, since the "eclipse" plumage attained following the postnuptial molt is usually less colorful and often quite femalelike.

Although in all the species which have so far been studied the female also has a comparable summer molt and plumage, in most cases this plumage is so similar to the winter plumage that separate descriptions are not necessary. In most cases the "eclipse" plumage of males is held for only a few months, presumably to allow the male to regain as early as possible the more brilliant plumage associated with pair formation. In some cases, however (e.g., ruddy duck, Baikal teal, blue-winged teal), this "nuptial" plumage is not regained until well into winter, and thus "summer" and "winter" plumages may be more or less recognizable. The situation is further complicated in the oldsquaw, which has a third partial molt in the fall (affecting both sexes but most apparent in the male) which is restricted to the scapular region. Except in such special cases, the two major plumages of the male are referred to in the species accounts as "nuptial" and "eclipse" plumages, while the "adult" plumage of females refers to both of the comparable breeding and nonbreeding plumages.

The 115 species of waterfowl that belong to the subfamily Anatinae are grouped into a number of tribes, most of which include one or more native North American species. The only major tribe of Anatinae that is not represented in this continent is the shelduck tribe Tadornini, which has representatives in both South America and Eurasia. It is true that there are some old records of Atlantic coast occurrences for the ruddy shelduck (*Tadorna ferruginea*) and the common shelduck (*Tadorna tadorna*), as well as a few more recent sight records (*Audubon Field Notes* 16:73; *American Birds* 26:842; 27:41), but these are quite possibly the result of escapes from captivity.

WOOD DUCK
Aix sponsa (Linnaeus) 1758

Other Vernacular Names: Carolina Duck, Summer Duck, Woodie.

Range: Breeds in forested parts of western North America from British Columbia south to California and east to Idaho, and in eastern North America from eastern North Dakota to Nova Scotia, south to Texas and Florida. Winters in the southern and coastal parts of the breeding range and southward into central Mexico.

Subspecies: None recognized.

IDENTIFICATION

In the Hand: Male wood ducks, even in eclipse plumage, can be recognized in the hand by their iridescent upper wing surface and long, squarish tail, which is also somewhat glossy. Unlike all other North American duck species, both sexes have a silvery white sheen on the outer webs of the primary feathers and a bluish sheen near the tips of the inner webs.

In the Field: Wood ducks sit lightly in the water, with their longish tails well above the surface. The birds are usually not found far from wooded cover. Often they perch on overhanging branches near shore and feed in fairly heavy woody cover that is flooded. The crest is evident on both sexes at a considerable distance, as is the male's white throat.

The brilliant color pattern of males in nuptial plumage is unmistakable. In the air, wood ducks fly with great ease and apparent speed, the bill tilted below the axis of the body and the head often turned, giving a "rubber-necked" appearance, while the long tail is also evident. The underwing surface is speckled with white and brownish, and the white on the trailing edge of the secondaries is usually apparent, as is the white abdomen. The male has a clear whistle with rising inflection, while the female utters a somewhat catlike and owllike sound, but no true quacking notes.

NATURAL HISTORY

Habitat and Foods. The preferred summer habitat of wood ducks consists of freshwater areas such as the lower and slower-moving parts of rivers, bottomland sloughs, and ponds, particularly where large hardwood trees are present. The birds nest in tree hollows (or substitutes such as nesting boxes) that have entrances about 4 inches in diameter, a cavity depth of about 24 inches, and a cavity bottom about 10 inches square. The birds seem to prefer cavities that are fairly high and which have small entrances, and also they prefer to nest among well spaced tree clusters or rows rather than in isolated trees. Nesting over water is preferred to dry-land sites, and additionally there must be brooding cover consisting of shallow water, dense overhead vegetation such as shrubs for hiding, and abundant foods such as insects and duckweeds. As adults, the birds have a tendency to forage on the nuts and fruits of woody plants, such as acorns and beechnuts, which are sometimes plucked directly from the trees or may be searched for among the forest litter. The birds also feed while swimming, but only rarely resort to diving while foraging.

Social Behavior. Wood ducks attain adult plumages and sexual maturity the first winter of life, and shortly after the males have completed molting into their nuptial plumages they begin social courtship. Displays in this species are conspicuous and have evolved to maximally display the crest, the brilliant body patterning, and the iridescent upperwing coloration. One of the most common male displays is a ritualized preening of the inner wing-feathers, producing a flash of secondary patterning that is directed toward a specific female. Females enter strongly into courtship by inciting males toward aggressive behavior among themselves, and gradually form pair bonds with specific males.

Breeding (hatched) and wintering (shaded) distributions of the wood duck in North America.

The bond lasts only through a single breeding season, but may be reformed the following fall if both birds come back into contact. Copulation in wood ducks is preceded by a prolonged period of male displaying while the female remains prone on the water, a situation quite different from the mutual precopulatory behavior of geese and of dabbling ducks.

Reproductive Biology. Most wood ducks have become paired by the time they return to their breeding areas, and these pairs soon begin to search for suitable nesting sites. Both sexes participate in the search, but the final choice of a site is evidently made by the female. In areas where suitable nest cavities are limited, competition over nest sites may result in more than one female wood duck laying her eggs in a single location, or in mixed clutches of wood duck and goldeneye or hooded merganser eggs. Even in normal clutches the number of eggs laid is surprisingly large; 13 to 16 eggs is probably a typical range. Incubation by the female begins with the last egg and requires about 30 days. During this period the male abandons his mate and, after moving into relatively heavy cover, begins his postnuptial molt. As soon as their young have left the nesting cavity by jumping to the ground a day or so after hatching, the females lead their broods to the nearest water. For the first two weeks of life they have little contact with other broods, but increasingly the young birds become amalgamated into groupings resulting from several broods. When they are about a month to six weeks old they are likely to be deserted by their mothers, who then begin their own molts. The young wood ducks fledge at about 60 days of age, and begin to form congregations, gradually moving to rivers and creeks that provide food and cover.

Conservation and Status. Although the wood duck was believed to be near extinction in the early 1900s, strong protective action and the innovative program of nesting-box erection undertaken by conservation agencies finally turned the tide, and in recent decades the species has not only become relatively abundant but also has spread its range west into areas of the Great Plains where it was previously virtually unknown. It is very difficult to judge total wood duck populations in North America, but the population in the eastern states and provinces was judged to be between 1.1 and 1.7 million birds in the 1960s and early 1970s. The west coast population is far smaller, but reliable figures are not available except for a wintering estimate of about 55,000 birds in 1960.

Suggested Reading. Grice and Rogers, 1965.

SURFACE-FEEDING DUCKS
Tribe Anatini

The surface-feeding, dabbling, or similarly described ducks are a group of about thirty-six species of mostly freshwater ducks that occur throughout the world. Many of them are temperate or arctic-breeding species that nest on dry land near freshwater ponds, marshes, rivers, or similar rather shallow bodies of water. Associated with this breeding habitat are their adaptations for foraging by "tipping-up" rather than by diving for food, an ability to land and take off abruptly from small water areas or land, and a moderately good walking ability but reduced perching capabilities as compared with perching ducks. Also unlike perching ducks, iridescent coloration on the wing is limited to the secondary feathers, or in rare cases is lacking altogether.

The surface-feeding ducks are among the most abundant and familiar of all North American ducks and include such popular sporting species as mallards, pintails, wigeons, and various teals. They range in size from less than a pound to more than three pounds and are among the most agile of waterfowl in flight, relying on maneuverability rather than unusual speed to elude danger. The number of North American breeding species is somewhat uncertain, but is at least nine. Additionally, the European wigeon very probably nests occasionally in continental North America, the Baikal teal is possibly a very rare nester, and the Bahama pintail breeds in the West Indies. Further, the "Mexican duck" is often considered to be a separate species from the common mallard, as are the populations called the Florida duck and mottled duck, so these might also be added, bringing the possible total to fourteen. Beyond these, the falcated duck is recognized by the A.O.U.

(1957) as belonging on the list of North American birds although there is no evidence for breeding, and in recent years there have been several sight records for the garganey, as well as an occurrence of the Chinese spot-billed duck (*Anas poecilorhyncha*) on Adak Island (Byrd *et al.*, 1974). Some of the records of falcated duck, Baikal teal, and garganey may well have been the result of escapes from captivity, but it seems likely that others of them represent wild birds, and thus these species are included in this book.

In most respects, the surface-feeding ducks closely resemble the perching ducks in their anatomy and biology, but differ from them in that they are nearly all ground-nesting species that are ill-adapted for perching. Although considerable diversity in bill shape exists among the surface-feeding ducks, most biologists now agree that recognition of a single genus (*Anas*) is most representative of the close relationships that exist among these species, rather than maintenance of the traditional separate genera for the shovelerlike ducks, the wigeons, and other subgroups. Similarly, it is quite clear that recognition of separate species of Old World and New World green-winged teals and species recognition for the endemic Mexican, Florida, and Gulf coast populations of mallards are not in keeping with the modern species concept of potentially interbreeding natural populations. Although such changes force some modifications of traditional vernacular names of these populations, these disadvantages seem minor compared to the distortions of natural relationships forced by the retention of traditional nomenclature.

EUROPEAN WIGEON
Anas penelope Linnaeus 1758
(Until 1973, regarded by the A.O.U. as *Mareca penelope*)

Other Vernacular Names: None in general use.

Range: Breeds in Iceland and the more temperate portions of Europe and Asia south to England, Germany, Poland, Turkistan, Altai, and northwestern Mongolia. Winters in Europe, northern and central Africa, and Asia. Regularly seen in fall, winter, and spring in North America, especially along the Atlantic and Pacific coasts, and most commonly seen in the interior during spring. Not yet determined to be a breeding species in North America, although such breeding seems probable.

Subspecies: None recognized.

IDENTIFICATION

In the Hand: Either sex may be safely distinguished in the hand from the American wigeon by the presence of dark mottling on the underwing surface, particularly the axillars. It may be distinguished from other surface-feeding ducks by the white to grayish upper wing coverts and the green speculum pattern, with a black anterior border. Both sexes are more brownish on the cheeks and neck than is true of the American wigeon.

In the Field: Females are not considered safely separable from the female American wigeon in the field, but if both species are together the more brownish and less grayish tones of the European species will be evident. Males in nuptial plumage are easily recognizable, since they exhibit a creamy yellow rather than a white forehead, and a cinnamon-red head and neck color instead of a light grayish one. Since some male European wigeon exhibit a green iridescence around and behind the eye, similar to that of the American wigeon, this is not a good field mark for distinguishing the two. The call of the male European wigeon is a shrill double whistle, sounding like *whee-uw*, while that of the American species is a series of weaker repeated single notes. Calls of the females are nearly identical. In flight, the mottled underwing coverts and axillars might be visible under favorable conditions.

AMERICAN WIGEON
Anas americana Gmelin 1789
(Until 1973, regarded by the A.O.U. as *Mareca americana*)

Other Vernacular Names: Baldpate, Widgeon.

Range: Breeds in northwestern North America, from the Yukon and MacKenzie regions east to Hudson Bay and south to California, Arizona, Colorado, Nebraska, and the Dakotas, with infrequent breeding farther east. Winters along the Pacific coast from Alaska southward to as far as Costa Rica, the southern United States, and along the Atlantic coast from southern New England south.

Subspecies: None recognized.

IDENTIFICATION

In the Hand: Apart from the European wigeon, American wigeon are the only surface-feeding ducks that have white or nearly white upper wing coverts, separated from a green speculum by a narrow black band. The rather short bluish bill and similarly colored legs and feet are also distinctive; only the pintail has comparable bill and foot coloration, and this species lacks pale gray or white on the upper wing coverts. See the European wigeon account for distinction from that species.

In the Field: American wigeon can be recognized on land or water by their grayish brown to pinkish body coloration. They often feed on land, eating green leafy vegetation, and float about buoyantly in shallow water, where they feed on aquatic leafy materials or steal it from diving ducks. The short bill and similarly short, rounded head are often evident, and when the male is in nuptial plumage his pure white forehead markings are visible for great distances, as are the large white areas on the sides of the rump, contrasting with the black tail coverts. The white upper wing coverts are usually not visible when the bird is at rest, but when in flight this is the best field mark, alternately flashing with the grayish underwing surface and with the white abdomen of both sexes. American wigeon are about the same size as gadwalls and often mix with them in flight. Both species have white underparts, but while the gadwall exhibits white at the rear of the wing only, the wigeon exhibits dark secondaries and white on the forward half. Males often call in flight or when on the water, uttering a repeated and rather weak whistle. Females are relatively silent ducks, and their infrequent, guttural quacking notes are not repeated in long series.

NATURAL HISTORY

Habitat and Foods. Breeding habitats of this species have never been accurately defined, but the birds seem to prefer rather shallow, semipermanent water areas, surrounded by hayfields or ungrazed woodlands for breeding. Areas having dry sedge meadows and in which most of the water surface is relatively open and free of emergent vegetation are especially preferred, as are those with a good development of such aquatic plants as water milfoil and pondweeds. Since wigeons do not dive for food it is important that vegetation can be reached easily by swimming birds. Additionally, wigeon are prone to graze along shorelines on grassy or sedge-covered meadow areas, and in some areas the birds also utilize such cultivated leafy crops as lettuce, alfalfa, and barley. On marine wintering areas they also forage on eelgrass and wigeon grass; muskgrass and wild celery are also preferentially consumed when they are available.

Social Behavior. American wigeon become sexually mature their first winter of life, and by midwinter the males will have molted into their first nuptial plumage and usually have also begun to participate in social display. Display in wigeon takes a form rather different from that

Breeding (hatched) and wintering (shaded) distributions of the
American wigeon in North America.

of other North American dabbling ducks. Females perform an inciting display that seems to provide the primary impetus for male courtship, but unlike typical *Anas* species the males do not perform elaborate posturing nor do they so frequently turn-the-back-of-the-head toward inciting females. Instead, they tend to face females, utter their loud and distinctive whistling calls, and variably raise their folded wings upward over their backs. They also perform display preening of their folded wings, and aerial chases are fairly frequent. Once formed, pair bonds persist through the nesting season, but the incidence of re-pairing with a mate of the previous season is probably rather low.

Reproductive Biology. By the time the birds have arrived on their breeding areas, nearly all of the females have established pair bonds, although this species is one of the last of the surface-feeding ducks to complete courtship activities. Females soon begin to seek out nesting sites, which often are relatively far from the nearest water, often in large stands of sedge meadows, or in mixed grass and herb cover. Sometimes the nest is placed at the base of a tree, and it is generally rather well concealed from above. The average clutch is of 9 or 10 eggs, and incubation lasts 23 to 24 days and is performed entirely by the female. Frequently males desert their mates almost as soon as incubation is begun, and rarely are they present after the second week of incubation. Males usually move to rather large marshes to complete their postnuptial molt, and as soon as the ducklings have hatched the females also move them to moderately large but shallow water areas. About 45 to 58 days are typically required to bring the young birds to fledging, although in Alaska it has been found that as little as 37 days may be needed, presumably because of the longer days at high latitudes and hence greater opportunities for continuous foraging. The female begins her own molt at about the time her brood is becoming independent, and as the young birds gain the power of flight they begin to assemble on marshes that provide a combination of protection from disturbance and abundant submerged aquatic foods.

Conservation and Status. Between 1955 and 1973 the breeding-season estimates of this species have ranged from 2.2 million to 3.1 million birds, making it one of the most numerous of North American ducks. It also ranks about fourth in numbers of ducks harvested in the United States and Canada. There is no indication that the species is in any special need of management or protection at the present time.

Suggested Reading. Keith, 1961.

FALCATED DUCK
Anas falcata Georgi 1775

Other Vernacular Names: Bronze-capped Teal, Falcated Teal.

Range: Breeds in central and eastern Siberia, probably west to the Yeni-
sei River, and southeast to Hokkaido in Japan. Winters in China,
Japan, and southeastern Asia south to Vietnam and upper Burma,
with occasional stragglers wintering in western North America, especially Alaska.

Subspecies: None recognized.

IDENTIFICATION

In the Hand: Both sexes of this rare dabbling duck are similar to
wigeon and also have a greenish speculum. But there is no black anterior border on the greater coverts, and the coverts are never pure
white, only grayish to grayish brown. The elongated sickle-shaped tertials
on the male are unique, and by themselves will identify that species, but
females lack these ornamental specializations. The brownish underparts of females, their longer culmen length (over 36 mm.), and the
presence of a rudimentary crest will serve to separate them from female
wigeon.

In the Field: Males in nuptial plumage, with their long, bronze- to green-glossed crest, "scaly" breast pattern, and long sickle-shaped tertials that nearly reach the water, are distinctive. The species is so rare in North America that lone females should not be identified in the field, since they closely resemble female wigeon and gadwalls.

GADWALL
Anas strepera Linnaeus 1758

Other Vernacular Names: Gray Duck.

Range: Breeds throughout much of the Northern Hemisphere, in North America from Alaska south to California and from Quebec south to North Carolina; also breeds in Iceland, the British Isles, Europe, and Asia. Winters in North America from coastal Alaska south to southern Mexico, the Gulf coast, and along the Atlantic coast to southern New England.

North American Subspecies:

A. *s. strepera* L.: Common Gadwall. Range as indicated above.

IDENTIFICATION

In the Hand: Positive identification of gadwalls in the hand is simple; they are the only dabbling ducks with several secondaries entirely white on the exposed webs, the remaining secondaries being black or grayish. Confirming criteria are the yellow legs and slate gray (males) or gray and yellowish (females) bill color, a white abdomen, and the usual presence of some chestnut coloration on the upper wing coverts.

In the Field: Although one of the easiest species of ducks to identify in the hand, gadwalls are perhaps the waterfowl most commonly misidentified or unidentified by hunters because of the species' lack of brilliant coloration. On the water, the male appears to have an almost entirely gray body, except for the black hindquarters, which are apparent at great distances. In spring, the upper half of the head appears to be a considerably darker shade of brown than the lower part of the head and neck, but during fall this difference is not so apparent. The female is best recognized by her association with the male, but at fairly close range the yellowish sides of her otherwise gray bill can be seen, and the bill is clearly shorter and weaker than that of a female mallard, which she closely resembles. The white secondaries are usually not visible when the birds are at rest. However, the white secondary pattern is highly conspicuous during flight, with white also appearing on the underparts of the body and on the underwing coverts, the rest of the bird appearing brownish. From early fall until spring the courting calls of the males can be heard, either when in flight or on the water, a combination of low-pitched *raeb* notes interspersed with *zee* whistles, often in a distinctive *raeb-zee-zee-raeb-raeb* cadence (on the water only). The female has various mallardlike quacking notes, including a series of paced *quack* notes when alarmed, or a decrescendo series of notes that are somewhat more rapid and higher pitched than occurs in mallards.

NATURAL HISTORY

Habitat and Foods. This widely distributed species of duck shows a preference for breeding on marshes or small lakes in grasslands, especially those having grassy islands providing safe nesting sites. Shallow semipermanent prairie marshes are preferred over deeper marshes, lakes, or temporary water areas, and nesting is most often done in heavy grass or weedy cover. In winter gadwalls are frequently found in freshwater areas and slightly brackish estuarine bays; in the former habitats they feed on pondweeds, water milfoil and wigeon grass, while in the latter they also consume wigeon grass, muskgrass, and other submerged aquatic plants. They are almost exclusively surface-feeders, and have only rarely been observed to dive for food. Thus, they are largely dependent on foods they can readily reach by tipping-up, and tend to feed in rather shallow marshes having abundant aquatic plant life growing close to the surface.

Social Behavior. Gadwalls become sexually mature and acquire their breeding plumages during the first winter of life. At least in the case of adult birds, social display begins surprisingly early, usually before the birds have fully molted out of their summer "eclipse" plumages.

Breeding (hatched) and wintering (shaded) distributions of the gadwall in North America.

It is likely that many of the early pair bonds thus formed are actually associated with the remating of previously paired birds, although this is yet to be proven. There is a secondary spring peak of social display, once again presumably resulting from the influence of young birds initially coming into breeding condition. Social display occurs both in the air and on water, and male posturing is both elaborate and fairly noisy. Several displays not occurring in the closely related wigeons but characteristic of most other *Anas* species are present, such as the "grunt-whistle," "head-up-tail-up," and "down-up." As in other surface-feeders, copulation is preceded by a rather prolonged period of mutual head-pumping, and is followed by the male calling once, and then turning to face the female in a motionless and erect posture.

Reproductive Biology. Shortly after pairs return to their breeding areas, they begin to fly out to grassy areas and search out nest sites. They prefer to locate their nests in dry, upland sites, amid dense cover that provides concealment on all sides and usually also from above. The nests are often at considerable distance from water, and during the egg-laying period the female will usually fly to a point up to 25 feet from the nest, and then walk in the remaining distance. A clutch averaging ten eggs is laid at the rate of one egg per day, with early clutches somewhat larger than later ones or ones resulting from renesting efforts. Males may desert their females as early as the seventh day of egg-laying, or may remain with her until the day before the eggs hatch, but they do not participate in nest defense or incubation. Following hatching, females with broods move to deep-water marshes and the edges of large impoundments, sometimes traveling more than a mile to do so. Fledging of the young occurs in 7 to 8 weeks, and during the last part of this period the female begins her own postnuptial molt.

Conservation and Status. The North American population of this widely spread species is probably quite large, averaging nearly 1.5 million in recent years. However, there have been substantial and unexplained regional variations in gadwall numbers, with the interior populations showing a consistent increase while the Atlantic coast population has declined and the Pacific coast birds have shown no consistent trends. The species is not very highly regarded by hunters, as it is considerably smaller than a mallard and lacks some of the beauty of plumage shown by other surface-feeding ducks. In any case, its population trends are not showing indications that the species is in need of special attention. Suggested Reading. Gates, 1962; Oring, 1969.

BAIKAL TEAL
Anas formosa Georgi 1775

Other Vernacular Names: Clucking Teal, Formosa Teal, Spectacled Teal.

Range: Breeds in eastern Siberia and northern Ussuriland, possibly also in Kamchatka. Some summer records from St. Lawrence Island, King Island, and mainland Alaska, but no established records of breeding. In winter found mainly in central China, with smaller numbers in Japan, Taiwan, and southeast Asia rarely as far as India, and with rare stragglers along the Pacific coast of North America to California.

Subspecies: None recognized.

IDENTIFICATION

In the Hand: Because of its very similar speculum pattern, the Baikal teal is most often confused with the green-winged teal, from which it can be readily separated by its longer tail (minimum 75 mm.) and larger size (over 14 ounces, or more than 400 grams). The male's distinctive head pattern is usually not attained until late winter, but the ornamental chestnut-striped scapulars and tertials are present earlier. Females should be carefully compared with the female green-winged teal, which they closely resemble, but differ in their definite white (rather than buffy and faintly striped) cheek spot at the base of the upper mandible, their clearer white throat with an extension up the sides of the cheeks, and the dark area above the eye that interrupts the pale superciliary stripe.

In the Field: The male in nuptial plumage is unmistakable at close range. The bird sits in the water with its colorful head low on the breast, its tail well out of the water, the ornamental scapulars hanging down over the flanks, and vertical white bars visible in front of the black under tail coverts and on the sides of the breast. Its distinctive clucking call, *ruk-ruk'*, or *ruk*, is uttered only during spring display. The quacking notes of the female are rather infrequent. In the air it resembles a green-winged teal, but has brownish gray rather than white underwing coverts. Lone females should not be identified as Baikal teal except under extremely favorable conditions, when their distinctive facial markings noted above can be clearly seen.

GREEN-WINGED TEAL
Anas crecca Linnaeus 1758
(Until 1973, regarded by the A.O.U. as *Anas carolinenis)*

Other Vernacular Names: Common Teal, Greenwing, Northern Green-winged Teal, Teal.

Range: Breeds throughout much of northern Europe and Asia, the Aleutian Islands, temperate North America, and Iceland. In North America, winters from southern Canada (along both coasts) through the central and southern states to Mexico and Central America.

North American Subspecies (recognized by Delacour, 1956):

A. *c. crecca* L.: European Green-winged (Common) Teal. Breeds in Iceland, Europe, and Asia. In North America, seen occasionally during winter, especially along the Atlantic coast.

A. *c. nimia* Friedmann: Aleutian Green-winged Teal. Resident in the Aleutian Islands, from Akutan westward.

A. *c. carolinensis* Gmelin: American Green-winged Teal. Breeds on the continent of North America, from north-central Alaska to New Brunswick and Nova Scotia.

IDENTIFICATION

In the Hand: This species is the smallest of the North American dabbling ducks, rarely if ever exceeding a pound (450 grams) in weight and having a tail of less than three inches (75 mm.). The bill is relatively long but unusually narrow (12-14 mm.). Besides this small size, the presence of a speculum that is green inwardly, black outwardly, narrowly edged behind with white, and with a brownish anterior border, is relatively diagnostic. A similar speculum pattern occurs only in the rare Baikal teal.

In the Field: Green-winged teal float lightly in the water, the tail usually well above the water, and males exhibit buffy yellow triangular patches on the black under tail coverts. The only white marking shown by males is the vertical bar in front of the gray sides (usually) or (in the rare European and Aleutian races) a horizontal white stripe between the back and flanks. In good light, the iridescent green head patch may be distinguished from the otherwise chestnut head, the two areas separated by a narrow and often faint (brighter in the European and Aleutian forms) buffy white stripe. Field recognition of the Aleutian and European races must be based on males; females can scarcely be distinguished in the hand. In the field, female green-winged teal may be identified by their small size, dark-colored bill, and brownish color, with the head showing a darker eye-stripe and a paler area near the base of the bill. In flight, green-winged teal are the essence of agility, twisting and turning like shorebirds, and alternately flashing their white underwing coverts and dark brownish upper wing. The dark upper wing color is perhaps the best way to separate green-winged teal from blue-winged or cinnamon teal, although green-winged teal also appear to have shorter necks and both sexes have pure white abdomens. During winter and spring the whistled *krick'-et* calls of the males can be heard almost as far away as the birds can be seen and often provide the first clue as to their presence in an area. The female has a variety of weak quacking notes and a decrescendo call of about four notes.

NATURAL HISTORY

Habitat and Foods. The green-winged teal has the broadest geographic range of any of the teal-size surface-feeding ducks, and breeds

Breeding (hatched) and wintering (shaded) distributions of the green-winged teal in North America. Horizontal hatching indicates breeding range of Aleutian green-winged teal.

over an array of habitats ranging from arctic tundra to prairies and semi-deserts. However, the highest nesting concentrations are associated with the wooded ponds located along the Canadian aspen parklands. Nesting frequently occurs there in grasses, sedge meadows, or on dry hillsides having brush or aspen cover, or sometimes in open woodlands near a pond or slough. Totally treeless or brushless habitats seem to be generally avoided. The foods of this tiny duck are relatively small seeds, small invertebrates, and the vegetative parts of aquatic plants. In the winter, green-winged teal are often found in tidal creeks or marshes associated with estuaries, and small mollusks are sometimes eaten in such locations, as well as the more typical aquatic plant materials.

Social Behavior. Like other *Anas* species, green-winged teal become sexually mature during their first winter of life, and a prolonged period of social display begins on wintering areas. This persists through the spring migration, and is completed about the time the birds return to their breeding grounds, which is relatively early. The sexual displays of the males are numerous and elaborate; groups of courting green-winged teal are notable for their animation and the rapidity with which one display follows another. Females perform inciting frequently during social display, and sometimes lead the males in erratic aerial chases. However, these flights apparently serve mainly to change the location of courting groups, and are probably not a fundamental part of pair formation. Copulation is preceded by a mutual head-pumping display. After treading, the male draws his head backward along the back in a "bridling" posture. Pair bonds are held only until incubation begins, and there is no information of the incidence of remating in subsequent seasons with past mates.

Reproductive Biology. Green-winged teal are among the earliest of spring waterfowl migrants, and arrive on nesting areas almost as soon as they become snow-free. Pairs soon begin nest-site searches, with the female making the final choice, while accompanied by her mate. Females usually line their nests with considerable amounts of down, and their nests are extremely well concealed, both from the sides and from above, in heavy grass, weeds, or brushy cover. The average clutch is about eight to ten eggs, laid at daily intervals. The incubation period of 21 to 23 days begins with the completion of the clutch, and males usually desert their mates at about the time incubation begins. Males may fly some distance to special molting areas before becoming flightless. Although the females are small and relatively defenseless, they care for and defend their broods with remarkable intensity. As a result, the duckling mortality rate is usually rather low, and many survive the approximately six-week period to fledging.

Conservation and Status. Because of the tiny size and the dispersal tendencies of this species, reliable information on population sizes and trends is almost impossible to obtain. Between 1955 and 1974 the estimated breeding population for North America averaged nearly 2 million birds, while an independent estimate based on banding and hunter-kill data in the mid-1960s suggested a total population of more than 3 million birds. Few hunters selectively hunt green-winged teal; their small size and elusive flight characteristics make them difficult targets.

Suggested Reading. McKinney, 1965.

COMMON MALLARD
Anas platyrhynchos Linnaeus 1758

Other Vernacular Names: Greenhead, Green-headed Mallard, Northern Mallard.

Range: Breeds throughout much of the Northern Hemisphere, in North America from Alaska to northern California and east to Ontario and the Great Lakes, with recent breeding extensions into New England. Also breeds in Greenland, Iceland, Europe, and Asia. Winters through much of the breeding range and south to extreme northern Mexico.

North American Subspecies (see also accounts of Mexican mallard, Florida mallard, and mottled mallard):

A. *p. platyrhynchos* L.: Common Mallard. Range as indicated above, except for Greenland.

A. *p. conboschas* Brehm: Greenland Mallard. Resident on coastal Greenland, with vagrant birds probably sometimes reaching continental North America.

IDENTIFICATION

In the Hand: The familiar green-headed and white-collared male in nuptial plumage needs no special attention, but females or immature males may perhaps be confused with other species. Except for the rare Mexican mallard, the presence of a bluish speculum bordered both in front and behind with black and white will serve to distinguish common mallards from all other North American ducks, with additional criteria being orange-colored legs and feet, a white underwing coloration, and a yellow to orange bill with varying amounts of black present. See the Mexican mallard account for distinction from that species, and the black duck account for recognition of hybrids.

In the Field: Mallards are large, surface-feeding ducks that exceed in size all dabbling ducks except the black duck. On the water, the dark, often apparently black, head color of the male is evident, as are the reddish brown chest and the grayish white sides and mantle, contrasting with the black hindquarters. More than any other dabbling duck, male mallards are dark at both ends and light in the middle. Females may be recognized by the combination of their fairly large size and their orange yellow bill, which is distinctly heavier and more orange than that of a female gadwall. Females also show a definitely striped head, with a dark crown and eye-stripe, contrasting with pale cheeks and a light superciliary stripe. The familiar, loud *quack* of the female is frequently heard, and her call consisting of a series of notes of diminishing volume is also commonly uttered. During aquatic display males utter a sharp whistled note, usually single but sometimes double, that can be heard for several hundred yards. Unlike many other dabblers, this courtship note is not uttered in flight. In flight, the male's immaculate white underwing coverts contrast with the female's brownish abdomen and upperparts. In the male the white of the underwing coverts is continuous with the whitish sides and abdomen and is terminated in front by chestnut and behind by black. The two white stripes associated with the speculum are also evident in flight.

NATURAL HISTORY

Habitat and Foods. Common mallards are perhaps the most adaptable of all duck species, as is attested by their broad range and relative abundance over most of the Northern Hemisphere. Because of this broad range, it is difficult to distinguish preferred nesting habitat from acceptable ones. However, mallards seem to prefer rather shallow marshes or ponds, where surrounding environments are not heavily forested, and they usually nest in fairly dry sites with rather tall grassy or herbaceous vegetation. The birds also accept a variety of winter habitats; a source of abundant food such as grain and a safe roosting site are minimal requirements. Saltwater areas are avoided, however, except in the Greenland population, where the birds have evolved unusually well developed nasal glands that allow them to consume salt water. In many areas of interior North America, agricultural grain crops such as corn have been exploited heavily, and in the southern states mallards are closely associated with rice fields. Important natural foods include wild rice, pondweeds, smartweeds, bulrushes, and many other submerged or emergent plants.

Social Behavior. Mallards become sexually mature rapidly, and young males may begin sexual display within four or five months of their hatching. Display occurs over a period of many months, frequently starting in September and persisting until May. Late courtship behavior is sometimes difficult to separate from behavior associated with attempted rapes of females by unpaired males; incubating females whose mates have deserted them are especially prone to such advances. Male displays are numerous and elaborate; the loud whistling notes associated with several of the displays can be heard for hundreds of yards. The incidence of remating with birds of the previous year is not yet well established, but one case in which two birds were known to be paired in each of five seasons has been documented. On the other hand, males who have left their females after incubation has begun will sometimes associate with or even attempt to rape other females.

Reproductive Biology. Mallards are extremely early spring arrivals on the northern nesting areas, and little time is wasted in selection of nesting sites by females. Nesting pairs establish rather large home ranges

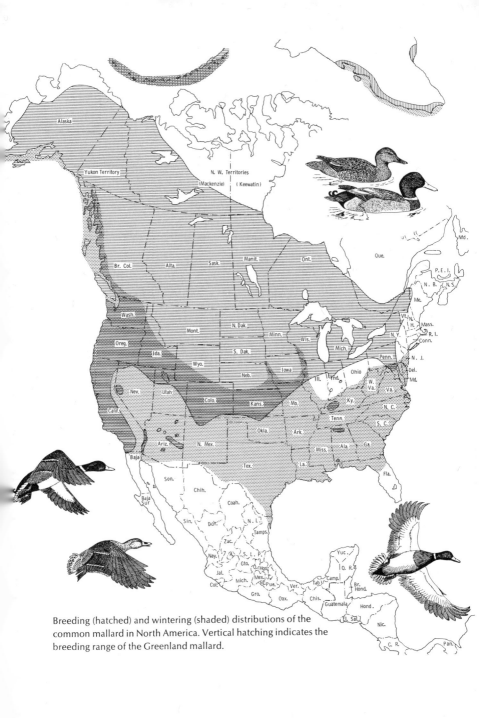

Breeding (hatched) and wintering (shaded) distributions of the
common mallard in North America. Vertical hatching indicates the
breeding range of the Greenland mallard.

that often exceed 700 acres, but within this area there is a central core of primary activity. Although mated males defend their mates from the attention of other males, no territorial boundaries in the usual sense are established, and thus females sometimes nest in rather close proximity to one another. They produce eggs at the rate of one per day until a clutch of 8 or 9 eggs is completed; early clutches may be slightly larger than this and late clutches or renests tend to be smaller. Incubation requires about 28 days, and about 30 hours are needed to complete pipping, or emergence of the duckling. Usually the first night after hatching is spent on the nest, after which the young are led to water. Females typically tend their broods for most of the eight-week period required for them to attain flight, and a few rare cases are known in which a female had laid a second clutch after successfully hatching an earlier one. Adults go through a flightless period of 24 to 26 days, with males molting about a month earlier than females that have hatched young.

Conservation and Status. The population status of the mallard is considered by many to be the most important indicator of the condition of waterfowl as a whole, since it is easily the most important sporting species of duck in North America. Fortunately, it responds well to management and breeds under conditions that would not be tolerated by many of the rarer species. Over the twenty-year period 1955-74 the breeding population in the continental interior averaged nearly 9 million birds, which perhaps represents about 84 percent of the total North American population. Thus, its condition might be considered as secure as that of any North American waterfowl species.

Suggested Reading. Coulter and Miller, 1968.

SOUTHERN MALLARDS
(Mexican, Florida, and Mottled Ducks)
(Anas diazi and A. fulvigula of A.O.U., 1957)

Other Vernacular Names: Dusky Mallard, New Mexican Duck, Summer Black Duck, Summer Mallard.

Range: Currently exists as three separate populations. One is resident in peninsular Florida from about Tampa on the west coast to the vicinity of Gainesville in the interior and Indian River on the east. Another breeds along the Gulf coast from the Mississippi Delta to central Veracruz (Johnsgard, 1961), wintering over most of the breeding range but probably undergoing some seasonal movements. The third is currently limited to a breeding range in the Rio Grande Valley of southern New Mexico, extreme southwestern New Mexico, and adjacent Arizona, and also occurs locally in Chihuahua, Durango, northern Jalisco, and the central highlands of Mexico south to the Trans-Mexican volcanic belt (Aldrich and Baer, 1970). Wintering occurs through much of the breeding range, but there is probably a partial movement out of the northernmost breeding areas in the United States (Johnsgard, 1961).

Subspecies:

A. *platyrhynchos diazi* Ridgway: Mexican Mallard. Range in New Mexico, Arizona, and Mexico as indicated above. The form *novimexicana* Huber is not recognized by Delacour (1956), Johnsgard (1961), or Aldrich and Baer (1970).

A. *p. fulvigula* Ridgway: Florida Mallard. Range in Florida as indicated above.

A. *p. maculosa* Sennett: Mottled Mallard. Range in the Gulf coast as indicated above.. This form is not recognized by Delacour (1956), although Johnsgard (1961) later concluded that it is probably a valid subspecies. The uncertainty of its validity makes a consistent method of providing suitable vernacular names for these populations impossible. If *maculosa* is eventually deemed invalid, the vernacular name "southern mallard" might best be applied to the populations now included in *fulvigula* and *maculosa*. Currently, neither the technical nor the vernacular names used by the A.O.U. (1957) provide a clear indication of the relative relationships of these forms to one another or to *platyrhynchos*, and the A.O.U. decision not to recognize vernacular names for subspecies tends to maintain an unwarranted degree of taxonomic separation of these populations.

IDENTIFICATION

In the Hand: Adult males are generally similar to females of the common mallard, especially *diazi*, which however are more heavily streaked and spotted with brown on the underparts and have unspotted yellow bills and (usually) black nails. Males of *maculosa* and *fulvigula* are generally darker and more tawny, with yellow to yellowish orange bills, black nails and a black mark near the base of the upper mandible. They also lack a definite white bar on the greater secondary coverts, since this area is suffused with tawny.

Females of all the populations are virtually identical to the males except for bill coloration. Females of *diazi* can be distinguished from female common mallards by one or more of the following traits: (1) the upper tail coverts are darker, with no patterning along the quill and with narrower light margins; (2) the outer tail feathers are darker, with little or no white present; (3) the under tail coverts are dark brown, with a lighter edging, instead of white with a central brownish stripe; (4)

the small underwing coverts are barred with brown; (5) the bill is darker, shading anteriorly to olive green with very little orange near the base; (6) the tertials are overlaid with a greenish cast; (7) the speculum is more greenish and has a reduced white border; and (8) the breast feathers usually are a darker brown, varying in pattern from three separate spots to a merged *fleur-de-lis* (Huey, 1961). Females of *fulvigula* and *maculosa* tend to be even darker than those of *diazi* and may have a more purplish speculum without a definite white anterior border.

In the Field: Birds of all three populations look very much like female common mallards in the field, but average variably darker in their plumage tones. The major difference is that *both* sexes have a yellow or olive bill color, with little or no dark spotting present, and when in flight the birds exhibit little or no white on their outer tail feathers. The body tones of *diazi* are sometimes only slightly darker than those of female common mallards, but females of *fulvigula* and *maculosa* are distinctly more tawny. These latter types also lack a definite white bar in front of the speculum. Female hybrids between common mallards and black ducks are very similar to females of these populations and are essentially impossible to distinguish in the field. Such hybrids do retain a small but distinctive white or grayish white bar on the greater secondary coverts, which would help to separate them from either Florida or mottled mallards, the only forms likely to be encountered where hybridization between common mallards and black ducks is most prevalent.

NATURAL HISTORY

Habitat and Foods. The nesting habitats of these mallardlike ducks are apparently much like those of common mallards: flat habitat having most of the land surface covered by wet prairies, seasonal marshes, and sloughs represents optimum nesting habitat by the Florida mallard, while the mottled mallard nests in salt marshes, coastal prairies, bluestem meadows, and fallow rice fields. Freshwater marshes with abundant emergent vegetation are also believed to be the preferential habitat of the Mexican mallard. Very little information is available on the foods of these populations, but in Florida it has been found that nearly 90 percent of the foods identified in one study were of vegetable origin. A variety of grasses, weeds, and sedges was present in these samples; like common mallards these birds seem to be rather opportunistic in the foods they consume.

Breeding distributions of the Florida (diagonal hatching), mottled (vertical hatching), and Mexican (horizontal hatching) mallards in North America.

Social Behavior. Although not all the populations have been studied, current information suggests that reproductive maturity is attained the first winter and that breeding occurs in yearlings, just as in common mallards. Likewise, the patterns of social display seem to be essentially identical to those of common mallards. The only possible difference that might be present in southern mallards is the potential for more or less permanent pair bonds to be established in these relatively sedentary birds with prolonged breeding seasons. At least in Florida mated pairs can be seen throughout the year, excepting only the brood-rearing period, and in Texas there seems to be a minimum of about 4 percent paired birds in the population during August.

Reproductive Biology. Dispersal of breeding pairs begins as early as February in Louisiana, and, like common mallards, rather large home ranges are soon established. In one study, these ranged from 105 to 327 acres among four pairs. The nest sites are established within the limits of the home range and, although normally well scattered, have been found as close as only 30 feet apart. Eggs are laid at daily intervals until a clutch averaging about ten eggs is completed. These southerly birds have a long potential breeding season and are persistent renesters when their initial breeding efforts fail; one mottled mallard in Texas was found to have made five nesting attempts before she finally successfully hatched a brood of nine ducklings. The incubation period is about 24 to 26 days, or slightly shorter than that of common mallards, and in some cases the pair bond seems to persist almost to the time of hatching. The female soon leads her ducklings to water, and a fledging period of 60 to 70 days is required to bring the young to flying condition, which is slightly longer than that for common mallards. Little information is available on behavior and movements of these birds in late summer, but the period of large flocking is rather limited, and at least in Texas the flocks have begun to break up into small units and eventually into pairs by November or December.

Conservation and Status. These populations of mallardlike ducks are rather difficult to census easily, in part because they are in large concentrations for so short a time. The Florida segment is believed relatively stable, and during the 1960s probably averaged about 50,000 birds. Likewise, the mottled duck has not shown any obvious trends, and during the breeding season probably consists of about 100,000 birds, while the fall population ranges from 200,000 to 250,000. The Mexican mallard is probably the least secure of the three, and only a few thousand birds probably exist north of the Mexican border, while prebreeding-season surveys in the mid-1970s suggested that there may be 30,000 to 40,000 birds present at the close of the breeding season. Habitat losses, and interactions with common mallards at the northern limits of the Mexican mallard's range, probably are the major threats to this form's survival.

Suggested Reading. Hubbard, 1977.

BLACK DUCK
Anas rubripes Brewster 1902

Other Vernacular Names: Black Mallard, Red-legged Black Duck.

Range: Breeds from Manitoba and Ontario eastward to Labrador and Newfoundland, south to Minnesota, and through the Great Lakes states to the Atlantic coast, where breeding occurs south to coastal North Carolina. Winters through the southern parts of the breeding range and south to the Gulf coast.

Subspecies: None recognized. Perhaps *rubripes* should itself be regarded as a subspecies of *platyrhynchos* (Johnsgard, 1961), in which case the vernacular name "black mallard" would be most appropriate.

IDENTIFICATION

In the Hand: Black ducks may be readily identified in the hand by their mallardlike shape and size, an almost entirely brownish black body color, and the absence of any white anterior to the speculum. Little or no white is normally present on the trailing edge of the secondaries, but hybridization with mallards has gradually diluted the purity of most black duck populations, so this criterion is not absolute. Female hybrids between mallards and black ducks most resemble mottled ducks, but usually show some white on the greater secondary coverts, especially on the outer web (Johnsgard, 1961). Male hybrids usually show some green iridescence behind the eyes, often forming a fairly distinctive green patch.

In the Field: The dark body with only slightly lighter head color makes black ducks conspicuous in any gathering of ducks. They are mallardlike in every respect except their coloration, including their vocalizations. In flight, the white underwing coverts contrast more strongly with the dark body and upper wing coloration than is true of mallards, and this flashing wing pattern of dusky and white makes black ducks recognizable for as far away as they can be seen. When in breeding condition, the brilliant yellow bill of the male is very conspicuous and allows for ready sexual identification.

NATURAL HISTORY

Habitat and Food. Largely limited to the eastern third of the United States and Canada, the black duck's preferred breeding habitat consists of forest environments where streams, bogs, swamps, or other water areas occur. Additionally, tidewater habitats provide nesting areas in the form of marshes and the margins of bays and estuaries, but these are used secondarily to the wooded environments. During winter, black ducks utilize marine habitats to a considerably greater degree than do mallards, and as a result their food intake tends to be higher in animal materials during that time of year than does that of mallards. However, in many areas black ducks have learned to utilize grain crops such as corn, especially where mallards and black ducks commonly associate.

Social Behavior. Like common mallards, black ducks mature their first winter, and from late fall through spring a substantial amount of time is spent in social courtship and pair formation. To a remarkable degree, displays, calls, and other aspects of behavior in the black duck are identical to those of mallards, and it is surprising that as little hybridization has occurred between them as the historical records suggest. At least until recent decades, a considerable separation existed in both breeding ranges and major wintering areas, but this has become increasingly blurred, and more social interactions between black ducks

Breeding (hatched) and wintering (shaded) distributions of the black duck in North America.

and mallards have developed. Mixed courtship groups, and subsequent mixed pairing and hybridization are thus fairly frequent in some areas and cast some fears on the future of the black duck as a distinct form. Hybrids appear to be as viable and as fertile as the parental species, and in a few areas may comprise as much as 5 to 10 percent of the combined population.

Reproductive Biology. Black ducks are early nesters, and females seek out sites that offer a high level of concealment while also providing a fairly dry substrate. The margins of wooded areas are highly preferred for nest locations. Island-nesting is not especially common in black ducks, except where sedge meadows or other marsh-nesting cover is not available. Eggs are laid at the rate of one per day, and an average clutch of nine to ten eggs is typical. As the breeding season progresses the average clutch size diminishes, and older females are known to produce larger average clutches than yearlings. Incubation requires about 27 days, and during the period of incubation males desert their mates. Unlike mallards, black ducks apparently do not often move to special molting areas, but instead become highly wary and are rarely seen during the month-long flightless period. About the time the young birds have completed their 7- to 8-week fledging period they are abandoned by their mothers, which then undergo their own postnuptial molts. Usually by late August both sexes are again flying and starting to gather with immature birds in favored foraging areas before their fall migration.

Conservation and Status. The recent history of the black duck in North America is an interesting and rather disturbing one. Not only has the total population undergone a prolonged decline of about 40 percent over the twenty-year period of 1955-74, there has also been an accelerating incursion of mallards into what were once prime black duck breeding and wintering areas. Although black ducks are probably able to hold their own in competition with mallards, the much larger gene pool of the latter makes it possible that the genetic integrity of black ducks might eventually be threatened by extensive hybridization with mallards.

Suggested Reading. Wright, 1954; Coulter and Miller, 1968.

BAHAMA PINTAIL
Anas bahamensis Linnaeus 1758

Other Vernacular Names: Bahama Duck, Bahama Teal, White-cheeked Pintail.

Range: The Bahama Islands, the West Indies, Colombia, eastern South America from Curaçao to Argentina, central Chile, and the Galapagos Islands, with rare stragglers reaching the southeastern United States.

North American Subspecies:
A. b. bahamensis L.: Lesser Bahama Pintail. The Bahama Islands, the West Indies, and northern and northeastern South America.

IDENTIFICATION

In the Hand: This dabbling duck could be easily confused only with the more common species of pintail, since both have elongated central tail feathers. However, the Bahama pintail's central feathers are of the same reddish buff color as the more lateral ones, and no other North American species of duck has white cheeks and throat, sharply contrasting with dark brown on the rest of the head. Likewise, the red marks at the base of the bluish bill are unique.

In the Field: The field marks for this rare but distinctive species are simple: a generally reddish brown duck with white extending from the cheeks to the base of the neck, red spots on the side of the bill, and a pointed tail. It is considerably smaller than the more common northern pintail, but has the same general body profile. In flight, it also exhibits a similar pattern of white, gray, and dark brown on the underwing coverts, but is otherwise much more reddish buff than the northern pintail. The male utters a weak *geeee* sound during courtship display, and the female's calls are scarcely distinct from those of the northern pintail.

Trumpeter Swan, Adult (drinking)

Lesser Snow Goose (Blue Phase), Adult and young

Lesser Canada Goose, Adults

Atlantic Brant, Adult

Barnacle Goose, Adults

Wood Duck, Adult Male

American Wigeon, Pair

Gadwall, Pair

Green-winged Teal, Pair

Mexican Mallard, Adult Male

Florida Mallard, Pair

Northern Pintail, Pair

Blue-winged Teal, Pair

Cinnamon Teal, Pair

Shoveler, Pair

Canvasback, Pair

Redhead, Pair

Ring-necked Duck, Pair

Greater Scaup, Pair

King Eider, Pair

Steller Eider, Adults

Oldsquaw, Pair

Harlequin Duck, Pair

Surf Scoter, Male

Bufflehead, Pair

Barrow Goldeneye, Pair

Common Goldeneye, Pair

Hooded Merganser, Displaying Male

Red-breasted Merganser, Male

Common Merganser, Pair

Ruddy Duck, Male

PINTAIL
Anas acuta Linnaeus 1758

Other Vernacular Names: American Pintail, Common Pintail, Sprig, Sprigtail.

Range: Breeds through much of the Northern Hemisphere, in North America from Alaska south to California and east to the Great Lakes and eastern Canada, in Greenland, Iceland, Europe, and Asia, as well as in the Kerguelen and the Crozet islands. Winters in the southern parts of its breeding range in North America, south to Central America and northern South America.

North American Subspecies:
A. a. acuta L.: Northern Pintail. Range as indicated above, except for the Kerguelen and the Crozet islands.

IDENTIFICATION

In the Hand: A pintail of either sex may be recognized in the hand by its slim-bodied and long-necked profile, sharply pointed rather than rounded tail, gray feet, gray to grayish blue bill, and a speculum that varies from brownish or bronze to coppery green, with a pale cinnamon anterior border and a white trailing edge. Another long-tailed species, the oldsquaw, has a large lobe on the hind toe, the outer toe as long or longer than the middle toe, and secondaries that lack iridescence or a white trailing edge.

In the Field: The streamlined, sleek body profile of pintails is apparent on the water or in the air. When on the water, males show more white than any other dabbling duck; their white breasts and necks can be seen for a half mile or more. When closer, the dark brown head, often appearing almost blackish, is apparent, as are the grayish flanks, separated from the black under tail coverts by a white patch on the sides of the rump. Females are somewhat smaller, mostly brownish ducks, with a dark bill that shows no trace of yellow or orange, and they show no conspicuous dark eye-stripe or pale spot on the lores as in some other female dabbling ducks. During winter and early spring, males spend much time in courtship display, and one of their distinctive courtship calls, a fluty *pfüh*, can often be heard before the birds are seen either in flight or on the water. The quacking notes of female pintails are not as loud as those of female mallards, and the decrescendo series of notes is usually rather abbreviated.

NATURAL HISTORY

Habitat and Foods. The breeding habitat of the pintail varies greatly throughout its enormous geographic range. In the arctic, this species is found in marshy, low tundra where shallow freshwater lakes occur, especially those with a dense vegetation along the shoreline. In general, it is associated with open, fairly flat terrain with shallow waters, swamps, bog lakes, and quiet rivers. Waters that are lined with trees are avoided, but on the other hand this bird is often associated with brushy thickets or aspen copses around sloughs in western Canada. Wintering habitats are also diverse, but in coastal regions the pintail favors shallow, fresh or brackish estuarine waters with adjacent agricultural areas that have scattered impoundments. Food during fall and winter is mostly of vegetable nature, mainly the seeds and vegetative parts of aquatic plants, emergents, and many terrestrial plants. Corn is a favored food wherever it is available, and large feeding flights to cornfields are characteristic in many parts of the country. Smaller grains are also utilized heavily, and possibly are preferred even more than corn.

Social Behavior. Pintails mature sexually in their first winter of life, and probably all females attempt to breed as yearlings. Pair formation

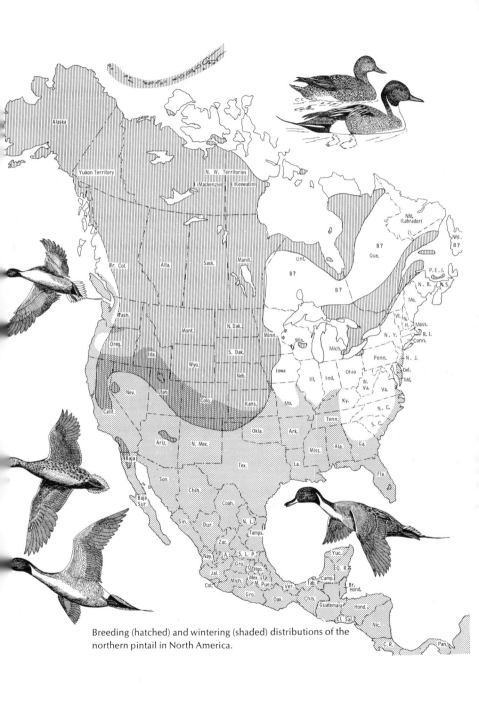

Breeding (hatched) and wintering (shaded) distributions of the northern pintail in North America.

occurs over a several-month period, starting on wintering areas in early December and continuing through the spring migration. Social display occurs primarily on water, although as the spring progresses an increasing number of spirited courtship flights and attempted rape flights can be seen in the northern states and Canadian provinces. Male displays are numerous, and the commonest is a vertical neck-stretching and associated fluty call called "burping." This is also often performed in flight, especially while females are uttering their inciting notes. Copulation occurs after a period of mutual head-pumping, and after treading is completed the male utters a burp-whistle while drawing the head back in a "bridling" posture.

Reproductive Biology. Pintails share with mallards the trait of arriving on their northern breeding areas before the ground has become completely snow-free, and they very soon set about dispersing over the available habitat. Dispersal is facilitated by the tendency for males to chase all females that intrude within their home ranges, although this behavior is not territoriality in the true sense. Since the birds are adapted to breeding in relatively upland situations, there is usually little crowding of nests. Frequently females establish their nest locations on sparsely vegetated hillsides a hundred yards or more from the nearest water. The average clutch is of about eight eggs, with the earliest clutches sometimes somewhat larger than this. Incubation begins with the laying of the last egg, and at about this time the males desert their mates and begin to congregate in favored molting areas around shallow, tule-lined sloughs and marshes. The fledging period of the young is from 40 to 46 days, or perhaps slightly less in the most arcticlike portions of the breeding range. This is perhaps the most northerly of all the surface-feeding ducks, even extending to 80° north latitude on Ellesmere Island. It's quite possible that some tundra-nesting pintails begin their southern migration before molting, to avoid spending the flightless period in the extreme north as fall is approaching.

Conservation and Status. Next to the mallard, the pintail is the second most abundant of North America's surface-feeding ducks, and at times its breeding population has been estimated in excess of 10 million birds. More generally, it has been closer to 5 million in recent years, but that is still enough to indicate that it is prospering over most of its range.

Suggested Reading. Sowls, 1978.

GARGANEY
Anas querquedula Linnaeus 1758

Other Vernacular Names: None in North America.

Range: Breeds from Iceland (rarely) to the British Isles, and from temperate portions of Europe and Asia to Kamchatka and the Commander Islands. In winter, found in southern Europe, northern and tropical Africa, southern Asia, and the East Indies, with stragglers very rarely occurring in Australia and North America.

Subspecies: None recognized.

IDENTIFICATION

In the Hand: This rare Eurasian duck is most safely identified in the hand, especially in the case of females. The garganey is a small dabbling duck with grayish upper wing coverts, a green speculum bordered narrowly behind and more broadly in front with white, and bluish gray bill and feet. Additionally, males not in eclipse exhibit a whitish superciliary line extending down the back of the neck, elongated scapulars ornamented with glossy black and white stripes, and blackish spots or bars on the brown breast and tail coverts. Females have a longer (at least 34 mm.) and wider bill than the green-winged teal, and show a more definite pale superciliary stripe and whitish cheek mark than either green-winged or blue-winged teal females.

In the Field: Females cannot safely be identified in the field, and the few North American records would demand specimen identification of females. Males in nuptial plumage are so distinctive, with their rich brownish head and white head-stripe, their scaly brown breast, gray sides, ornamental scapulars, and spotted brownish hindquarters, that field identification may be possible. In flight they most resemble blue-winged teal, having similar underwing coloration but grayish rather than bluish upper wing coverts. The voice of the male is a mechanical wooden rattling note, like that of a fishing reel. The female has an infrequent, weak, quacking voice.

BLUE-WINGED TEAL
Anas discors Linnaeus 1766

Other Vernacular Names: Bluewing, Teal.

Range: Breeds from British Columbia east to southern Ontario and Quebec, south to California and the Gulf coast, and along the Atlantic coast from New Brunswick to North Carolina. Winters from the Gulf coast south through Mexico, Central America, and South America, sometimes to central Chile and central Argentina.

Subspecies:

A. *d. discors* L.: Western Blue-winged Teal. Breeding range as above except for the Atlantic coast.

A. *d. orphna* Stewart and Aldrich: Atlantic Blue-winged Teal. Breeds along the Atlantic coast from southern Canada to North Carolina. Of uncertain validity; not recognized by Delacour (1956).

IDENTIFICATION

In the Hand: Blue-winged teal can be easily distinguished in the hand from all other North American ducks except perhaps the cinnamon teal. Any teallike dabbling duck with light blue upperwing coverts, a bill that widens only slightly toward the tip, and an adult culmen length of less than 40 mm. is probably a blue-winged teal. Males in nuptial plumage exhibit a white crescent on the face and white on the sides of the rump, but no cinnamon red body color. The females of blue-winged and cinnamon teal have overlapping measurements for both bill length and bill width, but the cinnamon has slightly longer soft flaps over the side of the mandible near the tip, producing a semi-spatulate profile when viewed from the side. Additionally, female blue-winged teal almost always have an oval area at the base of the upper mandible that is free of tiny dark spotting and thus appears light buffy to whitish, compared with the rest of the more brownish face. The same is true of the chin and throat, although the contrast is not quite so apparent. Spencer (1953) found that mandible length, but not its width, serves to separate these two species fairly well, as do differences in the shape of the lachrymal bone.

In the Field: On the water, blue-winged teal appear as small dabbling ducks with dark bills and generally brownish body coloration, the white facial crescent and lateral rump spot of the male being the only conspicuous field marks. Females have rather uniformly brown heads, without strongly blackish crowns or eye-stripes, but with a whitish or buffy mark just behind the bill. The bluish upper wing coverts are normally invisible on the water, but in flight these show up well and alternately flash with the underwing coverts, which are pure white except for a narrow anterior margin of brown. The call of the male is a weak, whistling *tsee* note, infrequently heard except during spring. The female has a high-pitched quacking voice and a poorly developed decrescendo call of about three or four notes, muffled at the end.

NATURAL HISTORY

Habitat and Foods. The preferred breeding habitats of the blue-winged teal are marshes in native prairie grasslands, especially the relatively wet tallgrass prairies. Additionally, locally wet areas of the drier shortgrass plains are used, as are the bunchgrass prairies of the Pacific Northwest. In coastal areas, breeding occurs in salt-marsh meadows with adjoining ponds or creeks. Wintering habitats in the United States are almost nil, since nearly all the birds migrate southward out of the colder parts of North America into Mexico, Central America, and South America. The annual food intake of the blue-winged teal is about three-fourths vegetable matter, and seeds constitute an important element among the plant materials, although vegetative parts of many different

Breeding (hatched) and wintering (shaded) distributions of the blue-winged teal in North America.

aquatic plants are also consumed. These small surface-feeding ducks seem to be extremely reluctant to dive for their food, and thus tend to concentrate on shallow waters where they can easily feed by simply tipping-up.

Social Behavior. This species matures in the first winter of life, and flocking persists through the spring migration. This is partly because of the rather late molt and correspondingly late onset of social display, and additionally blue-winged teal are among the latest of the surface-feeding ducks to begin nesting. Pair bonds are developed gradually during the period of social display, which consists primarily of aggressive chin-lifting displays by the males and associated calling. Likewise, inciting by females has a strong chin-lifting component, which is sometimes confused with precopulatory head-pumping but which occurs in very different social situations. Besides chin-lifting, males also perform several aquatic displays that mostly consist of ritualized forms of foraging behavior. Little actual courtship occurs in the air; short "jump-flights" are used by males to attract the female's attention and perhaps get closer to her, but many of the more prolonged chases evident late in spring on the breeding grounds are attempted rape chases rather than true courtship flights.

Reproductive Biology. Shortly after their arrival on the breeding grounds, males of paired birds become increasingly intolerant of one another and direct their attacks toward the females of other pairs. Yet, there is no real evidence that anything like typical territoriality occurs in this species, even though interpair aggression may serve to disperse the breeding pairs widely over the available habitat. Females soon seek out suitable nesting sites, generally picking locations that represent dry sites in undisturbed grass cover up to about 2 feet in height. They avoid both unusually tall cover and steep slopes, and nests frequently are on slightly rolling land, about halfway between water and the highest surrounding point of the land. The clutch is laid at the rate of one egg a day, and in early nesting tends to be between ten and twelve eggs. Later nests and renesting efforts have substantially smaller clutches, averaging only about five or six eggs. Incubation lasts 21 to 23 days, and during that period the male abandons his mate to begin the postnuptial molt. The young fledge in six to seven weeks, and during the latter stages of brood-rearing there frequently is a considerable amount of brood-merging. After leaving his mate, the male moves to suitable molting cover and becomes flightless for a period of three to four weeks.

Shortly after regaining their ability to fly, males begin to leave the breeding areas, followed in a few weeks by females and recently fledged young. *Conservation and Status.* Ranking third, behind the mallard and pintail, in population of surface-feeding ducks, the blue-winged teal has had an average breeding-season population of about 5 million birds during the period 1955-1974. Although the long-term welfare of this species largely depends on the abundance of prairie "potholes" and semipermanent marshes in the upper plains, which are vulnerable to drainage and disturbance, there has not been a serious decline in numbers in recent years.

Suggested Reading. Dane, 1966.

CINNAMON TEAL
Anas cyanoptera Vieillot 1816

Other Vernacular Names: None in general use.

Range: In North America, breeds from British Columbia and Alberta southward through the western states as far east as Montana, Wyoming, western Nebraska, western Texas, and into northern and western Mexico. Also breeds in northern and southern South America. The North American population winters in the southwestern states southward through Mexico, Central America, and northwestern South America.

North American Subspecies:

A. *c. septentrionalium* Snyder and Lumsden: Northern Cinnamon Teal. Breeds in North America as indicated above.

IDENTIFICATION

In the Hand: The rich cinnamon red color, the reddish eyes, and the lack of white on the body distinguish the male cinnamon teal from the only other teallike duck with blue upper wing coverts, the blue-winged teal. Females are much more difficult to identify, but if the bill is fairly long (culmen length of 40 mm. or more), somewhat wider toward the tip, and the soft lateral margins of the upper mandible distinctly droop over the lower mandible toward the tip, the bird is most probably a cinnamon teal. Unlike female blue-winged teal, female cinnamons have yellowish rather than whitish cheeks with fine dark spotting extending to or nearly to the base of the bill, eliminating the pale mark or at least making it smaller than the size of the eyes. Likewise, fine dark spotting on the cinnamon teal extends farther down the chin and throat, restricting the size of the clear throat patch. Duvall (cited by Spencer, 1953) found that twenty-six female blue-winged teal had a maximum exposed culmen length of 41 mm., while seventeen female cinnamon teal had a minimum exposed culmen length of 41 mm., with means of 38.7 and 43 mm., respectively.

In the Field: Female cinnamon teal cannot be safely distinguished from female blue-winged teal except under the best conditions and by experienced observers. Their smaller cheek spot, more rusty body tone, and longer, somewhat spatulate bill are most evident when both species are side by side. However, males can be recognized, even when in full eclipse, by their reddish to yellowish eyes, and when in full nuptial plumage their coppery red body color is unique among North American ducks. The vocalizations of the females of the two species are nearly identical, but male cinnamon teal have a low, guttural, and shovelerlike rattling voice, which is uttered during courtship display. In flight, the male's reddish underpart and upperpart coloration, relieved by the light blue upper wing covert pattern, is easily recognized, but the females cannot be distinguished from female blue-winged teal. Normally, females closely associated with males of either species can be safely assumed to be of the same species.

NATURAL HISTORY

Habitat and Foods. Like the blue-winged teal, cinnamon teal prefer to nest in open country dominated by fairly low herbaceous cover, especially grasses, and near shallow water areas, particularly rather alkaline ponds or marshes. Small and shallow areas receive higher use than do large and deeper ones, although brood-raising seems to be done on ponds that have both open water zones and considerable emergent vegetation. Most wintering occurs south of the limits of the United States, mainly

Breeding (hatched) and wintering (shaded) distributions of the
cinnamon teal in North America.

in western Mexico, where these birds are rather common in many coastal areas. Relatively little is known of their diet, but it probably differs but slightly from that of the blue-winged teal. It is known that the seeds and vegetative parts of pondweeds, and the seeds of bulrushes, salt grass, and sedges are important summer and fall foods.

Social Behavior. Cinnamon teal mature sexually in their first year of life, and so far as is known all yearling females attempt to breed. Like blue-winged teal, they molt into nuptial plumage relatively late, and courtship display continues at an intensive level through spring migration and for a time after arrival on the breeding grounds. Male display is very much like that of the blue-winged teal and northern shoveler, being dominated by aggressive chin-lifting postures toward other males, and submissive or sexual posturing toward females, particularly ritualized foraging postures. As in other *Anas* species, the combination of female inciting and turning-the-back-of-the-head by males seems to be a fundamental aspect of pair bonding. Although pair bonds are terminated during the nesting period in North America, some of the tropical populations of this species in South America have a much more prolonged breeding season and it is possible that relatively permanent pair bonding may be present in those populations.

Reproductive Biology. Female cinnamon teal construct a rather simple nest of dead grasses and plant stems, usually in vegetation about a foot in height and having good to excellent concealment characteristics. The first few eggs may be deposited at intervals of one to three days, but later ones are usually laid at a daily rate. The clutch size is normally between nine and eleven eggs in early or initial nesting efforts, and as many as three attempted nestings have been documented in a single season. The incubation lasts 21 to 25 days, and during this period the male deserts his mate. The males apparently do not collect in large groups during the molting period, and begin to move southward almost as soon as they have again regained the power of flight. The ducklings fledge in approximately seven weeks, and they too waste little time in starting their southward migration. This sometimes occurs with remarkable speed; an immature female banded in Utah in late July was shot near Mexico City in mid-August, indicating an average minimum movement of more than 100 miles a day.

Conservation and Status. Since almost all cinnamon teal winter outside the United States, the annual winter surveys are of no value in judging this species' population size or trends. However, breeding season surveys have suggested that about 260,000 birds occur in the western states and British Columbia. Without better information, it is impossible to judge whether the species is increasing or declining in numbers.

Suggested Reading. McKinney, 1970; Spencer, 1953.

NORTHERN SHOVELER

Anas clypeata Linnaeus 1758
(Until 1973, regarded by the A.O.U. as *Spatula clypeata*)

Other Vernacular Names: Shoveller, Spoonbill, Spoonbilled Duck.

Range: Breeds through much of the Northern Hemisphere, including
the British Isles, Europe except for northern Scandinavia, most of
Asia except for the high arctic, and in ·North America from western
and interior Alaska southward to California and eastward to the Great
Lakes, with some breeding along the middle Atlantic coast.

Subspecies: None recognized.

IDENTIFICATION

In the Hand: The strongly spatulate bill, which has soft lateral
margins near the tip that hang over the sides and obscure the long lamellae, is unique to the shoveler among North American species of
waterfowl. Additionally, the light blue upper wing coverts and the orange
legs and feet are distinctive.

In the Field: Whether on the water or in the air, the long, spoon-
like bill of both sexes is easily apparent, being distinctly longer than the
head and destroying the otherwise fairly sleek lines of the duck. Males

do not acquire their striking nuptial plumage until rather late in the winter, so that during fall most shovelers are femalelike in appearance, with the enlarged bill and bluish upper wing coverts being the primary field marks, the latter normally visible only when the bird is flying. In flight, the underwing surface is entirely white, and the underparts of females or dull-plumaged males are brownish, so that from underneath the birds distinctly resemble female mallards except for the more prominent bill. During late winter and spring the males acquire a white breast, a large white area between the black tail coverts and the reddish brown sides, and an iridescent green head. At this time they are reminiscent of male mallards, except that the breast is white and the sides reddish brown, instead of vice versa. Males are quite silent except during aquatic courtship, when low-pitched rattling notes are uttered. The female has a quacking voice similar to those of cinnamon and blue-winged teal, and her decrescendo call is usually about five notes long, with the last one or two rather muffled.

NATURAL HISTORY

Habitat and Foods. Shallow prairie marshes are the preferred breeding habitat of shovelers, particularly marshes with abundant plant and animal life floating on the surface, such as duckweeds and associated biota. Deeper prairie marshes are used to a lesser extent, although those supporting submerged aquatics such as pondweeds and water weeds are valuable as brood-rearing habitats. Open rather than wooded shorelines are preferred by shovelers for nesting, and in coastal areas the birds sometimes nest where freshwater ponds or shallow shorelines for feeding are available. In the winter, shovelers tend to be well distributed on fresh- as well as brackish-water habitats, but are more localized in salt-water situations. Feeding throughout the year is done essentially at the surface, by straining out small plankton-sized organisms with the long lamellae of the oversized bill. In this way aquatic insects, insect larvae, and other invertebrates such as crustaceans and mollusks are obtained, as well as duckweeds. Additionally, the vegetative parts of pondweeds, wigeon grass, and other submerged aquatics are eaten, as are the seeds of bulrushes, pondweeds, and the like.

Social Behavior. Shovelers mature in the first winter of life, and gradually the males develop the brilliant nuptial plumage associated with courtship display. Courtship continues at a high intensity through

Breeding (hatched) and wintering (shaded) distributions of the
shoveler in North America.

the spring migration, and even upon arrival at the breeding grounds the females are sometimes still unpaired or only weakly paired. Social display consists of aggressive chin-lifting displays among the males, turning-the-back-of-the-head by males toward females, and several sexual displays derived from foraging postures. Copulation is preceded by mutual head-pumping behavior, and is terminated by the male calling while assuming a rigid posture beside the female, with the body fairly erect and the bill pointed diagonally downward. Once pair bonds have been formed they tend to be quite strong, and may persist until hatching or even somewhat afterward.

Reproductive Biology. Shovelers are moderately late in returning to their breeding grounds, and seem to be in no rush about starting nesting; they may begin to look for suitable sites as early as 27 days before the start of egg-laying. They tend to select upland sites in cover less than a foot high, and frequently more than 100 yards away from the nearest water. About a week may be spent in nest construction, after which eggs are laid at the rate of one per day until a complete clutch of eight to ten eggs is present. Although the male remains with his mate well into incubation and sometimes after hatching, the female increasingly remains on the nest as incubation progresses. Hatching typically occurs after 22 to 25 days, with about 12 hours usually elapsing between the pipping and hatching of individual eggs. The brood normally leaves the nest within 24 hours of the completion of hatching, and frequently moves to several different ponds during the fledging period, which varies from about six weeks in the southern part of the range to as short a period as 36 days in Alaska.

Conservation and Status. Perhaps because of its rather specialized foraging adaptations, the shoveler is not nearly so common as some of the other species which, like it, have ranges extending across much of the Northern Hemisphere. Breeding population estimates of the 1950s and 1960s have averaged about 1.9 million birds, but whereas the species seems to have increased in the interior of the continent it has declined in the Atlantic flyway. It is not a popular bird with sportsmen, and thus hunting cannot be blamed for these changes, which more likely reflect general ecological trends in the habitats used.

Suggested Reading. McKinney, 1967, 1970.

POCHARDS (Fresh Water Diving Ducks) Tribe Aythyini

Until recent classifications by Jean Delacour and others, the pochard group was not taxonomically distinguished from the more marine-adapted sea ducks, here included in the following tribe Mergini. Nevertheless, the pochards are a readily definable group of mostly medium-sized ducks that differ from their close relatives, the surface-feeding ducks, in several respects. Their legs are situated somewhat farther back on the body, so that they are less adept at walking on land; their feet and associated webs are larger, increasing diving effectiveness (reflected by the increased length of the outer toes); and their bills are generally broad, heavy, and adapted for underwater foraging. Depending on the species, the predominant food may be of animal or vegetable origin. Internally, the males have tracheal tubes that are variably enlarged, and in contrast to the typically rounded and entirely bony structure of the tracheal bulla, this feature is angular and partially membranaceous. No iridescent speculum is present on the wings, but in many species the secondaries are conspicuously white or at least paler than the rest of the wing. The birds nest closely adjacent to water and sometimes even above the water surface, on reed mats or similar vegetation.

North America has five well-distributed species of pochards, one of which (the greater scaup) also extends to the Old World. Additionally, North American tufted duck records have become so numerous in recent years that the inclusion of that species has seemed necessary. One other Old World species, the common pochard (*Aythya ferina*), has rarely occurred in Alaska, with several Aleutian Islands records in recent years (Byrd *et al.*, 1974).

CANVASBACK
Aythya valisineria (Wilson) 1814

Other Vernacular Names: Canvas-backed Duck, Can.
Range: Breeds from central Alaska south to northern California and
east to Nebraska and Minnesota. Winters from southern Canada
south along the Atlantic and Pacific coasts to central and southern
Mexico.
Subspecies: None recognized.

IDENTIFICATION

In the Hand: Canvasbacks are the only North American pochards
that have a culmen length in excess of 50 mm. (or two inches); additionally the bill is uniquely sloping from its base to the tip and lacks a
pale band near the tip. Supplementary criteria include the presence of
vermiculated upper wing coverts, with the white predominating over
the dark, rather than the darker tones predominating.

In the Field: When on the water, male canvasbacks appear to be nearly white on the mantle and sides, whereas male redheads are distinctly medium gray, and the longer, more sloping head of the canvasback is usually evident. Compared to the redhead, the head is a duller chestnut brown, darker above and in front of the red eyes; in redheads the head is a more coppery red and little if at all darker in front of the yellow eyes. Female canvasbacks are distinctly longer-bodied than female redheads and lighter in brownish tones, with a brown breast usually distinctly darker than the more grayish sides, whereas in redheads the difference in color between the breast and the flanks is not very apparent. Both sexes appear longer-necked than redheads; in males this is accentuated by the extension of the reddish brown color beyond the base of the neck. In flight, this difference is also apparent; the black breast of the male canvasback is more restricted and does not reach the leading edge of the wings, whereas in redheads the black breast extends to the front of the wings. In females the brownish breast appears sharply separated from the pale grayish sides, while in female redheads the brown breast color is continuous with the brown of the sides and flanks. Except during courtship, canvasbacks are relatively quiet, but the male's cooing courtship call (uttered only on the water) may be heard frequently during the spring.

NATURAL HISTORY

Habitat and Foods. The preferred breeding habitat of canvasbacks consists of shallow prairie marshes surrounded by cattail, bulrushes, and similar emergent vegetation, large enough and with enough open water for easy takeoffs and landings, and with little if any wooded vegetation around the shoreline. Although most of the canvasback's prime nesting habitat lies in the northern plains states and prairie provinces, its major wintering habitat is associated with coastal bays, particularly Chesapeake Bay on the Atlantic coast and San Pablo Bay in coastal California. Optimum wintering habitat consists of fresh and brackish estuarine bays with extensive beds of submerged plants or abundant invertebrates, especially certain thin-shelled clams and small crabs. Beds of wild celery in freshwater habitats are heavily utilized by canvasbacks, as are pondweeds, wigeon grass, and eelgrass in the more brackish areas. Pondweeds and wild celery are also probably the most important foods in the interior of the continent, and lakes or marshes with heavy growths

Breeding (hatched) and wintering (shaded) distributions of the canvasback in North America.

of these plants often provide major concentration points for canvasbacks.

Social Behavior. Although canvasbacks become sexually mature in their first winter in life, it is by no means certain that all females nest when yearlings. As in other pochard species, there seems to be a proportion of the females that do not even attempt to nest each year, and presumably these are yearling birds. However, probably all form pair bonds, during a prolonged period of social display that begins on the wintering grounds and often continues for some time after arrival on the breeding areas in spring. Much of the display occurs on water, and consists of several postures and dovelike calls on the part of the males. Basically the same array of postures is shared by all members of the genus *Aythya*, but the associated calls, the plumages exhibited, and the relative speed and amplitude of the movements vary greatly among the various species. Thus, even the closely related redhead differs considerably in its display details from the canvasback, and very few hybrids have been reported between these species, even in captivity.

Reproductive Biology. Female canvasbacks intensively seek out nest sites in marshy areas, often spending considerable time in the effort and sometimes abandoning one or two nests before settling on a final location. Thus, the first eggs may be "dropped" before the nest is completed, and sometimes these eggs are "parasitically" placed in the already constructed nests of other marsh-nesting waterfowl, including other canvasbacks. Redheads likewise both commonly receive canvasback eggs in their nests and frequently place theirs in the nests of canvasbacks. From the time the clutch is completed, which usually consists of nine or ten eggs in nonparasitized nests, the female canvasback rather rarely leaves her nest. The incubation period normally lasts about 24 days, but sometimes as long as 29 days. The inclusion of eggs laid by other females sometimes confuses the incubation period and may result in several unhatched eggs being left in the nest at the time of general hatching. Following hatching, the female takes her brood from the nest to the open water of larger ponds and lakes. By that time the males have already begun their postnuptial molt and flightless period, and it is usual for females to also abandon their broods before they have fledged to begin their own molt. Fledging requires about 56 to 68 days, and this rather long fledging period probably places a limit on the northerly range of the species.

Conservation and Status. The canvasback has undergone several periods of reduced populations in this century, of which the drought period of the 1930s was one of the most serious. Additionally, in the 1960s a second period of very unfavorable breeding conditions resulted in hunting restrictions, and in the early 1970s it was estimated that the breeding populations were probably only about a half-million birds, doubtless including a substantial number of nonbreeders. Many causes of this serious decline in canvasbacks can be cited, including habitat loss, local over-hunting, and the like, and of all the major North American game waterfowl the canvasback is perhaps the most seriously theatened with possible eventual extinction.

Suggested Reading. Hochbaum, 1943.

REDHEAD
Aythya americana (Eyton) 1838

Other Vernacular Names: Red-headed Duck, Red-headed Pochard.

Range: Breeds from central Canada southward to southern California, New Mexico, Nebraska, and Minnesota, with local or occasional breeding farther east. Winters from the southern part of its breeding range from Washington eastward to the middle Atlantic states and south to the Gulf coast of Mexico and Guatemala.

Subspecies: None recognized.

IDENTIFICATION

In the Hand: Easily recognized as a pochard by its lobed hind toe and generally broad, flattened bill; redheads are typical of this genus of diving ducks. Males in nuptial plumage may be identified by their uniformly coppery red head and yellow eyes and by their flattened bluish bills with a pale subterminal band and a blackish tip. The black breast and the uniformly gray speculum, of nearly the same color as the upper wing coverts, are similar to those of the canvasback, but the black breast extends from the wings to the foreneck, and the upper wing coverts are slightly darker rather than lighter than the secondaries. Females may be separated from female canvasbacks by their shorter bills and more rounded head profile (see canvasback account) and from female ring-necked ducks by their longer wings, black margined inner secondaries, less definite eye-rings and eye-stripes, and the usual white flecking on their scapulars (see ring-necked duck account).

In the Field: On the water, redheads appear to be shorter-bodied and shorter-necked than canvasbacks, and have a shorter and more rounded head profile. Males have a brighter, more coppery head color, and the backs and sides of the body are medium gray rather than whitish, while female redheads are more uniformly brownish on the head, breast, sides, and back, lacking the two-toned effect of female canvasbacks. During late winter and spring, the male courtship call of redheads is frequent and audible for long distances; it is a unique catlike *meow* sound that few would attribute to a duck. Like most pochards, females rarely utter loud calls that are useful for field identification. In flight, male redheads appear mostly grayish to white from underneath, except for the black breast (which extends back to the leading edge of the wings) and brownish head. Their shorter necks and greater amounts of black on the breast are the best means of distinction from male canvas-backs. Females likewise exhibit white on the abdomen and the under-wing surface, and the brown color of the head and breast extends back in an unbroken manner under the wings along the sides. Redheads fly with strong rapid wingbeats, in a swift flight with relatively little dodging or flaring such as occurs in dabbling ducks, and they are more agile in flight than canvasbacks.

NATURAL HISTORY

Habitat and Foods. Prime redhead breeding habitat consists of nonforested country with water areas sufficiently deep to provide per-manent, fairly dense emergent vegetation as nesting cover. Water areas of at least an acre are preferred, especially areas with about 10 to 25 percent of the habitat consisting of open water for taking off and land-ing. Although species of plants are not critical, hardstem bulrush is a favorite nesting cover. During the winter, redheads move toward the coast, and concentrate on large bodies of water near the coastline that

Breeding (hatched) and wintering (shaded) distributions of the redhead in North America.

are fairly shallow and protected from heavy wave action, and which contain beds of submerged aquatic plants such as pondweeds, wigeon grass, and wild celery. Foods consumed are essentially identical to those of canvasbacks, but redheads tend to utilize somewhat more alkaline or brackish waters than does that species. The leaves, stems, seeds, and rootstalks of aquatic plants are all consumed, and in summer a fairly substantial amount of animal food in the form of aquatic invertebrates is also eaten.

Social Behavior. Redheads attain their adult plumages and become sexually active their first winter of life, although the incidence of non-nesting or parasitic nesting by yearling females is still uncertain. In any case, probably all females establish pair bonds during winter and spring, during a period of intensive display that occurs on the water and involves several male displays and calls. Females initiate display by inciting behavior, and males respond with neck-stretching, head-throwing, and other postures, and with associated catlike calls. Aerial chases, involving tail-pulling of the female by the chasing males, are often seen on the breeding grounds but are rare during migration, suggesting that they do not play a role in the pair-forming process, which is nearly completed by the time birds arrive on their breeding grounds. Copulation, as in all pochards, is preceded by bill-dipping and preening movements on the part of the male and sometimes also the female, and is followed by the male uttering a single "kinked-neck" call and then swimming away from the female in a rigid bill-down posture.

Reproductive Biology. Females may begin nest-building from two days to a week before egg-laying begins. Social parasitism plays a significant role in the breeding biology of redheads, and apparently a considerable number of females never build nests at all but rather simply deposit their eggs in nests of other marsh-nesting waterfowl, especially other redheads, canvasbacks, and ruddy ducks. Eggs are laid at the approximate rate of one per day, and the parasitically laid eggs have a lower hatching success than those which are incubated by the female that laid them. Incubation requires about 24 days, and before its completion the males desert their mates and begin their postnuptial molt. Not only do redheads have a rather low hatching success as a result of nest desertion and the influence of parasitically laid eggs, but they also are relatively poor parents, often abandoning the brood while the latter are relatively young and still unable to fly. The fledging period is probably between 56 and 73 days, and the young birds often soon stray rather far from the areas where they were hatched. Young birds and females are highly vulnerable to hunting mortality, which is one of the many serious conservation problems concerning this species.

Conservation and Status. Like the canvasback, the redhead has suffered serious population losses over the last few decades, and during the period 1955–1974 the breeding populations have averaged about 650,000 annually. Habitat losses, low reproductive success resulting from high predation rates by raccoons and other nest predators as well as from the species' generally inefficient reproductive behavior, and hunting mortality have all contributed to this population trend, which is a serious threat to the species.

Suggested Reading. Weller, 1959.

RING-NECKED DUCK
Aythya collaris (Donovan) 1809

Other Vernacular Names: Blackjack, Ring-billed Duck, Ringbill, Ring-neck.

Range: Breeds from Mackenzie District through the forested regions of southern Canada, south locally to California, Colorado, Nebraska, Iowa, Pennsylvania, and New York, and from New England to Nova Scotia, Cape Breton Island, and Newfoundland. Winters along the Pacific coast from British Columbia to Baja, California, in most of Mexico and adjoining Central America, in the southeastern states and along the Atlantic coast north to Massachusetts, and in the West Indies.

Subspecies: None recognized.

IDENTIFICATION

In the Hand: Ring-necked ducks are often misidentified by hunters, the males usually being confused with scaup and the females with scaup or redheads. The pale whitish ring near the tip of the bill will separate both sexes from scaup, as will the absence of predominantly white secondary feathers. The male ring-necked duck may be readily distinguished from redheads or canvasbacks by its darker, rather glossy greenish black upper wing coverts and tertials, which lack any light gray vermiculations. Females, however, are much more difficut to separate, for although ring-necks lack the long, sloping bill of female canvasbacks, redheads also have a whitish band near the tip of the bill. Nevertheless, unlike female redheads, female ring-necked ducks have secondaries that are more distinctly grayish than are the relatively brown coverts, and a white eye-stripe and eye-ring are more evident. The wings are shorter (folded wing less than 200 mm. vs. at least 210 mm. in female redheads), and the scapulars are never flecked or vermiculated with whitish.

In the Field: When in nuptial plumage, the male ring-necked duck on the water is the only North American diving duck that has a black back and breast pattern, with a vertical white bar extending upward in front of the folded wing. The rare tufted duck also has a black back and breast, but lacks the white bar and has a much longer and thinner crest than does the ring-neck. The ring-neck's white ring near the tip of the bill is often apparent at close range, but the chestnut ring at the base of the neck is rarely visible. Females on the water are probably best identified by their association with males, but usually exhibit a white eye-ring and posterior eye-stripe, as well as the white ring near the tip of the bill. Females lack the scaup's white facial mark, but they do have distinctly pale areas near the base of the bill. In flight, ring-necked ducks resemble scaup but lack white wing-stripes, and their darker back and upper wing coloration serves to separate them from redheads or canvasbacks, even before the head coloration is apparent. Ring-necks are relatively quiet ducks, and the courting calls of the male include a soft breathing note and a louder whistling sound difficult to characterize, both of which are only uttered on the water.

NATURAL HISTORY

Habitat and Foods. The favored breeding habitat of this species consists of sedge-meadow marshes and bogs, particularly the latter. The presence of water lilies and surrounding heather cover such as sweet gale or leatherleaf seems to be an integral part of the species' habitat. Thus, this species tends to be associated with coniferous forests rather

Breeding (hatched) and wintering (shaded) distributions of the ring-necked duck in North America.

than open prairie marshes, and in this way differs considerably from its close relatives. In the winter, the birds remain partial to shallow, acid marshes, but also use coastal lagoons, where they tend to avoid the more saline areas. Throughout the year they are essentially vegetarians, in this way resembling canvasbacks and redheads and differing from the superficially similar scaups. The seeds of water shield, and the seeds and vegetative parts of pondweeds and other submerged or emergent aquatic plants are their primary foods, with animal materials comprising only from about 10 to 25 percent of the total diet. These birds tend to feed in shallower water than do other diving ducks, and remain submerged for relatively short periods when foraging.

Social Behavior. Although it is assumed that ring-necked ducks are ready to breed when yearlings, since they form pair bonds and assume nuptial plumages the first winter of life, captive females infrequently lay their first year, and it is possible that a substantial amount of nonbreeding may also occur in wild female yearlings. Nonetheless, sexual display is a conspicuous part of the social behavior of flocks during winter and spring. The displays are quite similar to those of redheads and canvasbacks, but the associated vocalizations are weak and the posturing is not so extreme, and thus display is easily overlooked by the casual observer. A very soft whistling note accompanies some of the male postures, and inciting is the primary female display. Copulation is preceded by the usual bill-dipping and preening displays, which in this species seems to be performed by females as well as males.

Reproductive Biology. Females apparently are responsible for selecting the nest site, but are accompanied by males on their nest-hunting excursions. In early-nesting birds, as much as a week or ten days may elapse between the selection of a site and the laying of the first egg, while late-nesting birds may begin to lay almost immediately. Sometimes little or no actual nest is evident at the time the first egg is deposited, but down is gradually added and the vegetation overhead may be woven together to form an overhead arch. Nests may be either on ground or over water in emergent vegetation, but most frequently are on floating islands, with hummocks another preferred location. Most importantly, the site must be fairly dry, with suitable cover, and quite close to water of swimming depth. The clutch is usually of about nine eggs, which are laid at the rate of one per day. During the last two weeks of incubation the females rather infrequently leave the nest, and during this period the male usually abandons his mate. Hatching typically occurs on the

26th or 27th day of incubation, and most eggs hatch within a six- to eight-hour period. The female then normally broods her young for at least twelve hours before leaving the nest permanently. The fledging period is 49 to 56 days, which is rather short for pochards, and typically females remain with their broods this entire period, even if they themselves have become flightless.

Conservation and Status. Although once apparently less widespread, the ring-necked duck in recent decades has colonized many new breeding areas, especially in the northeastern states. Between 1953 and 1973 the annual survey data indicated that an average of nearly half a million ring-necked ducks were present on the breeding grounds, and although both breeding season and winter surveys indicate large annual variations in these numbers no consistent population trends are evident.
Suggested Reading. Mendall, 1958.

TUFTED DUCK
Aythya fuligula (Linnaeus) 1758

Other Vernacular Names: None in North America.

Range: Breeds in Iceland, the British Isles, and through most of northern Europe and Asia to Kamchatka and the Commander Islands. Winters in central and southern Europe, northern Africa, southern Asia, the Philippines, and Japan, with stragglers regularly appearing on both the Pacific and Atlantic coasts of North America and rarely inland.

Subspecies: None recognized.

IDENTIFICATION

In the Hand: This rare Eurasian duck has been seen frequently enough in North America to warrant a knowledge of its identifying marks. The bill is slightly narrower and shorter than that of a scaup (maximum culmen length 42 mm.; maximum width under 24 mm.) and is only slightly wider toward the tip than at the base, while both the nail and adjacent tip are black in color. Whitish vermiculations are lacking on the back and upper wing coverts of both sexes. Males have a thin, drooping crest, which is rudimentary in females, but females lack a white cheek mark large enough to be continuous across the forehead (some females have a whitish mark at the sides of the mandible).

In the Field: Females may not safely be distinguished from female scaup in the field, but males may be safely recognized by the presence of a black back and chest with no white vertical bar between them (eliminating ring-necked ducks) and a thin, drooping crest on a purplish head (eliminating scaups). In flight, both sexes are very similar to scaup and cannot be safely distinguished from them by inexperienced persons. The calls of both sexes are virtually the same as those of the scaup.

GREATER SCAUP
Aythya marila (Linnaeus) 1761

Other Vernacular Names: Big Bluebill, Bluebill, Broadbill.

Range: Breeds in Iceland, in northern Europe and Asia to northern Siberia, and in North America from arctic Alaska and arctic Canada east to the eastern shore of Hudson Bay, to northern Labrador, Anticosti Island, and Newfoundland. In North America winters on the Pacific coast from the Aleutian Islands to California, on the Gulf coast almost to Mexico, on the Atlantic coast from Florida to southern Canada, and on the eastern Great Lakes.

North American Subspecies:

A. *m. mariloides* (Vigors): Pacific Greater Scaup. Breeds in North America as indicated above, as well as in eastern Asia. Includes *nearctica*, which is recognized by the A.O.U. (1957) as the North American breeding form.

IDENTIFICATION

In the Hand: As with the lesser scaup, the presence of a white speculum, a bluish bill which broadens toward the tip, yellowish eyes, and vermiculated gray to brownish upperparts will eliminate all other species of ducks. For separation from lesser scaup, see the account of that species.

In the Field: In good light, male greater scaup exhibit a greenish, rather than purplish, gloss on the head and have a relatively low, uncrested head profile. Additionally their back appears more grayish, since it has a more finely vermiculated pattern. In flight, the extension of the white speculum to several of the inner primary feathers may be apparent. Female greater scaup are difficult to distinguish from female lesser scaup unless they are together. They are slightly larger and have more white on the face, especially on the forehead. The calls of the females of both species are similar, the most frequent one a low, growling *arrrr* that is somewhat weaker in the lesser scaup. The courtship calls of the male greater scaup are a very soft, cooing *wa'hoooo* and a weak and very fast whistle *week-week-week*, compared with the lesser's faint *whee-ooo* and a single-noted *whew* whistle (Johnsgard, 1965). In both species these calls may only be heard at fairly close range during courtship activity.

NATURAL HISTORY

Habitat and Foods. The preferred breeding habitat of the greater scaup consists of tundra, or low forest closely adjacent to tundra. In general the species seems to require relatively open landscapes, cool temperatures, and shallow, highly productive waters having open, preferably grassy, shorelines. Like many other waterfowl, greater scaup show an affinity for nesting among colonies of gulls or terns, and additionally prefer to nest on water areas having small islets with grassy or herbaceous cover. Outside of the breeding season, the birds tend to be distinctly maritime, and in winter seek out brackish or salt estuarine bays or marine bays. At those times they forage almost exclusively on animal materials, especially mussels and clams. Likewise, spring and summer foods are also high in animal materials; only in fall does vegetable matter such as the seeds and vegetative parts of submerged plants seem to comprise an important part of the diet.

Social Behavior. Although it is clear that greater scaup attain adult plumage and form pair bonds during the first year of life, it is by no means certain that all yearling females attempt to nest. However, courtship occurs over a long period in winter and spring, and involves both first-winter and older birds. It is marked by intensive inciting behavior

Breeding (hatched) and wintering (shaded) distributions of the greater scaup in North America.

on the part of females, and by the same displays in males as occur in lesser scaups and other pochard species. Indeed, the plumages and displays of lesser and greater scaups are so similar that hybridization between the two species would surely be prevalent were it not for the fact that they tend to be ecologically separated during the pair-forming period. Likewise, the behavior associated with copulation in lesser and greater scaups is nearly identical.

Reproductive Biology. Apparently pair bonds are relatively strong in greater scaup, frequently persisting until well into the incubation period. Females choose nesting sites that are typically hidden in grass growth of the previous year, often in rock cracks and fairly close to water. Easy access to water and fairly good visibility are probably important criteria in site selection, and cover provided by herbaceous growth and low shrubs is also favored. Frequently nests are situated very near one another, and such close proximity also facilitates nest parasitism. Clutches that are not affected by parasitically laid eggs average about 8 or 9 eggs, although parasitized ones or dump nests may have as many as 21 eggs. The incubation period is about 24 or 25 days, although some estimates of 28 days have been made. Following hatching, the young scaup feed mainly on the surface, catching floating insects or those flying just above the surface. Thus the weather shortly after hatching, including its effect on insect abundance as well as its chilling effects on the young, is critical to duckling survival. This is especially the case in coastal nesting areas, where the young are typically moved into the deeper waters of coastal bays shortly after hatching, and are directly exposed to the elements. The fledging period is still uncertain, but probably is no less than the approximately 45- to 50-day fledging period of the lesser scaup.

Conservation and Status. The greater scaup is far less abundant in North America than is the lesser scaup, and breeding-grounds counts in Alaska during the period 1957-1973 suggest an average breeding season population of about 500,000 birds. Canada also supports a relatively small number of breeding greater scaup, perhaps no more than 100,000 birds. Similarities between the two scaup species make it impossible to survey accurately or to determine if the greater scaup is increasing or declining at present.

Suggested Reading. Weller *et al.*, 1969.

LESSER SCAUP
Aythya affinis (Eyton) 1838

Other Vernacular Names: Bluebill, Broadbill, Little Bluebill.

Range: Breeds from central Alaska eastward to western Hudson Bay and southward locally to Idaho, Colorado, Nebraska, and the Dakotas. Winters from British Columbia southward along the Pacific coast to Mexico, Central America, and Colombia, and on the Atlantic coast from Colombia north to the mid-Atlantic states, as well as in the West Indies.

Subspecies: None recognized.

IDENTIFICATION

In the Hand: Lesser scaup are best separated from greater scaup in the hand, and even then some specimens may remain doubtful. In the case of females, the presence of a white facial mark and white on the outer webs of the secondaries will exclude all species but the greater scaup. Female lesser scaup usually have no white on the inner webs of any primaries, although some may be quite pale. The length of the culmen in female lesser scaup is 36 to 40 mm., while female greater scaup have culmen lengths of 41 to 46 mm. Female lesser scaup rarely exceed 2 pounds, but female greater scaup average more than 2 pounds. Males can usually be distinguished from greater scaup by a purplish rather than greenish gloss on the head, a more extensive area of grayish vermiculations on the back, no definite white on the vanes of the primaries (although the inner ones may be quite pale), culmen length of 38 to 42 mm. (vs. 43 to 47 mm.), a nail width of less than 7 mm. (vs. 8 or more), maximum bill widths of 20 to 24 mm. (vs. 22 to 26 mm.), and a maximum weight of 2.5 pounds (vs. an average weight of about 2.5 pounds). The bill of the lesser scaup also tends to have a more concave culmen profile and to be relatively narrower at the base than that of the greater scaup.

In the Field: Male lesser scaup, when seen in good light, show a purplish gloss on the head and have a higher head profile, with a rudimentary crest usually evident, rather than a green-glossed head and a low head profile. The back of the male lesser scaup also appears more speckled, since the vermiculations in these areas are coarser. In flight, the restricted amount of white on the wings may be evident. Females cannot be safely separated in the field, but those of the lesser scaup do tend to show less white in front of the eyes than do female greater scaup.

NATURAL HISTORY

Habitat and Foods. The preferred breeding habitat of lesser scaup consists of prairie marshes or potholes and partially wooded "parklands." Shallow lakes and ponds having low islands, moist sedge meadows, and brushy cover or stands of bulrushes along the shore are highly preferred, especially if they support abundant invertebrates, such as aquatic insect larvae and amphipods ("scuds"). In the winter, the birds concentrate on fresh to brackish estuarine bays, sometimes moving into salt estuarine bays, especially during severe weather. Winter concentrations are largely associated with the distribution of animal foods such as mollusks and fishes. On the breeding grounds amphipod crustaceans are the most important single food source, while during fall migration mollusks appear to predominate. The plants that are consumed are essentially the same as those of other pochards, particularly the seeds and vegetative parts of pondweeds, wigeon grass, and other submerged aquatics.

Social Behavior. It is clear that scaup become sexually active in the first winter of their lives, but apparently yearling scaup are less

Breeding (hatched) and wintering (shaded) distributions of the
lesser scaup in North America.

inclined to breed and less likely to breed successfully than are older females. Social display occurs commonly in the large flocks of wintering birds, and continues with high intensity through the spring migration. The associated displays are much like those of the other pochards, of which the most elaborate is an extremely rapid head-throw, associated with a soft whistling call. The focal point of male display is directed toward inciting females, and spirited chases through the air, above the water surface, and sometimes even below the surface are a common feature of spring courting activity. During pair-bonding behavior a considerable amount of display preening occurs, which exposes the conspicuous white speculum pattern. Preening of the wing or the dorsal region is also part of the precopulatory display behavior of the male and sometimes also the female.

Reproductive Biology. The lesser scaup is one of the latest of the prairie-nesting ducks to begin nest-building and egg-laying, although the advantages of such late nesting remain obscure. The birds typically choose nest sites on dry land, often on islands with grassy or herbaceous cover, but floating sedge mats are also highly utilized when they are available. Eggs are laid at a daily rate, with an average of ten eggs in complete clutches. However, repeated renesting is fairly common, and as many as four nesting efforts in a single season have been documented. The incubation period is about 23 to 25 days, and males usually desert their mates at about the time incubation begins. Following hatching the brood is taken to the relatively open water of large marshes. Females take fairly good care of their offspring, and sometimes two females will care jointly for their merged broods, with one remaining behind to threaten or feign injury when danger arises while the other leads the combined brood to safety. The fledging period is probably about 50 days, with some birds remaining flightless until late August or even early September.

Conservation and Status. Unlike most of the other pochard species, the lesser scaup has remained abundant and widespread as a breeder, and has shown no obvious downward trends in the past few decades. The average annual breeding season population of nearly 7 million scaup in North America for the period 1955 to 1975 is comprised mostly of this species, making it one of the most abundant of North American waterfowl.

Suggested Reading. Gerhman, 1951; Rogers, 1964.

SEA DUCKS
Tribe Mergini

The sea ducks are mostly arctic-adapted diving ducks that usually winter in coastal waters and typically breed in tundra situations or in northern forests. All twenty species (two of which are now extinct) depend predominantly or exclusively on animal sources of food, such as shellfish, mollusks, other invertebrates, and aquatic vertebrates such as fish. In general the sea ducks are thus not regarded as highly as table birds as are the surface-feeding ducks and some of the more vegetarian pochard species. Like the pochards, their legs are placed well to the rear and their feet are unusually large; thus the birds have sacrificed the ability to walk easily for their diving adaptations. Also in common with pochards, their generally heavier bodies relative to wing surface area prevent them from taking flight without running some distance over the water before reaching minimum flight speed. In the air they often make up in speed for their limited maneuverability, although some of the largest sea ducks are rather ponderous in flight. Some species exhibit a good deal of white on the wings while in flight, and, unlike the pochards, two species have iridescent speculum patterns. The arctic-breeding and tundra-nesting forms typically build open-cup nests in low vegetation, while the forest-nesting species often use hollow trees or other natural cavities. Some of these tree-nesting species have moderately long tails and can perch fairly well, but the larger eiders and scoters rarely stray far from the water's edge and are rather helpless on land.

North America is well endowed with fifteen extant breeding species of sea ducks, and the now extinct Labrador duck once ranged along the Atlantic coast from Labrador to Chesapeake Bay. Further, the Old World smew has been reported several times in recent years, so that of

the twenty species of sea ducks, the only species not reported from North America are two Southern Hemisphere mergansers and an Asian species of merganser. Most of the North American species also occur extensively in the Old World, with the bufflehead, surf scoter, Barrow goldeneye, and hooded merganser being the exceptions.

COMMON EIDER
Somateria mollissima (Linnaeus) 1758

Other Vernacular Names: American Eider, Northern Eider, Pacific Eider.

Range: Breeds in a circumpolar distribution on Greenland, Iceland, the British Isles, Scandinavia, Novaya Zemlya, northeastern Siberia, and Kamchatka; and in North America from the Aleutian Islands and the Alaska Peninsula to western and northern coastal Alaska, the arctic coast of the Yukon and the Northwest Territories and offshore islands, Hudson Bay, Labrador, Newfoundland, the Gulf of St. Lawrence, New Brunswick, Nova Scotia, and coastal Maine. In North America, winters in coastal areas of the Pacific south to Washington and along the Atlantic coast south to the middle Atlantic states, with casual occurrences inland.

North American Subspecies (based on Delacour, 1959):

S. *m. borealis* (Brehm): Northern Common Eider. In North America breeds from Greenland and northeastern Canada to northern Hudson Bay, where it intergrades with *dresseri*.

S. *m. dresseri* Sharpe: American Common Eider. Breeds in southern Labrador, Newfoundland, the Gulf of St. Lawrence, Nova Scotia, and Maine. Also breeds in southern Hudson Bay and James Bay, a population recognized by the A.O.U. as S. *m. sedentaria* Snyder and probably a valid race, but not recognized by Delacour.

S. m. v-nigra Bonaparte: Pacific Common Eider. In North America, breeds from northern Alaska east to Coronation Gulf and the Northwest Territories, and south to the Aleutian Islands, Kodiak Island, and the south side of the Alaska Peninsula to Cook Inlet and Glacier Bay.

IDENTIFICATION

In the Hand: In the hand, specimens may be immediately recognized as eiders by the somewhat sickle-shaped tertials and the irregular basal feathering of the bill, plus the rather large body that usually weighs in excess of three pounds. The common eider differs from all other eiders in having a lateral extension of feathering on the side of the bill that tapers to a point below the rear tip of the nostrils and an unfeathered extension of the bill that extends nearly to the eyes; these are present in both sexes and all ages. The bill color and the width of this unfeathered extension toward the eyes varies with different subspecies. Should the bill and head characteristics not be available for observation, the combination of brown barring on the sides or mantle and a folded wing length greater than 250 mm. will separate female common eiders from spectacled eiders. For adult males, the presence of white or mostly white tertials and a folded wing length in excess of 270 mm. will separate common eiders from spectacled eiders and king eiders.

In the Field: On the water, common eiders may be recognized at great distances by the male's white mantle color, which extends downward on the breast to the anterior base of the wings. King eiders have a black mantle, and spectacled eiders have blackish color extending partway up the breast toward the front of the neck. Female common eiders are less rusty-toned and paler than female king eiders and are vertically barred with dark brown rather than having crescentic brown markings. In flight, common eiders fly in a straight course with strong wing strokes; the males exhibit a continuous white mantle between their white upper wing coverts and have a black crown-stripe that is lacking in the other eiders. Male common eiders utter rather loud cooing sounds during courtship similar to those of mourning doves, but lack the tremulous quality of king eider calls. Female calls are loud and hoarse, often sounding like *gog-gog-gog*, and lack the wooden tone of king eider calls.

NATURAL HISTORY

Habitat and Foods. The preferred breeding of common eiders consists of low-lying rocky marine shores having numerous islands; there is also rare utilization of sandy islands and of coastal freshwater lakes or rivers. Boulder-strewn islands with grassy rather than wooded vegetation are preferred for nesting, and proximity to marine food is a basic breeding habitat requirement. Outside of the breeding season common eiders are almost entirely maritime birds, usually remaining well offshore and generally out of sight from land. At that time their major foods (mollusks and some crustaceans) certainly determine their distribution patterns. The birds typically forage just beyond the surf, diving and detaching mussels from rocky bottoms, and foraging especially at low tides and during daylight hours. At night they move farther out into the open ocean, sometimes several miles from their foraging areas.

Social Behavior. Common eiders attain essentially their full nuptial plumages in their second winter of life, and active courtship display initially occurs at that age. There has been some doubt about whether two-year-old eiders breed, but it seems likely that at least some females of that age-class do attempt to nest. Courtship in common eiders is marked by intensive inciting behavior on the part of females and a rather complex and unpredictable series of calls and postures by males, which generally may be classified as "cooing movements." Soft, dovelike calls are uttered as the neck and head are moved, and different subspecies vary to some extent in their display repertoire and in the frequency with which particular displays are performed. Copulation is preceded by the female's assumption of a prone position while the male performs a prolonged series of displays, including displays given during courtship as well as many postures derived from preening, bathing, and other comfort movements.

Reproductive Biology. Upon return to their nesting areas, female eiders begin to seek out nest sites that are sheltered by rocks and in flat open and grassy areas. Rock overhangs and well-drained ridges that become snow-free early in the season are also preferred locations. The birds tolerate a high level of crowding, and in dense colonies on small islands there may be as many as 100 nests or more in areas of 1,000 square feet. Before the start of incubation the pair may spend a good deal of time resting on communal loafing areas, and males visit the actual

Breeding (hatched) and wintering (shaded) distributions of the
common eider in North America. Horizontal hatching indicates
breeding range of Pacific, vertical hatching northern, and
diagonal hatching American common eiders.

nest site only during the period of egg-laying. The clutch size of common eiders varies somewhat with latitude, being largest at the middle latitudes, but is typically between four and six eggs. The incubation period lasts 25 to 30 days, apparently varying somewhat with population or degree of disturbance. One or two additional days are needed to complete hatching and the drying of the young, which then are led to tidal pools. At first the ducklings feed almost entirely from the surface, but they gradually gain in diving efficiency. As they develop, a tendency for brood merger becomes increasingly evident, and large clutches of ducklings typically form. The fledging period is probably from 60 to 75 days, perhaps varying regionally or with subspecies.

Conservation and Status. No figures are available on the entire North American population of common eiders, but it is possible that Alaska supports about 100,000 common eiders during summer, most of which are of the Pacific race. Probably at least that many also nest in western Canada. As many as half a million eiders have been found wintering off the Massachusetts coast, which all presumably nest in eastern Canada and Greenland, so perhaps a total of a million or more may be reasonable.

Suggested Reading. Cooch, 1965.

KING EIDER
Somateria spectabilis (Linnaeus) 1758

Other Vernacular Names: None in general use.

Range: Breeds in a circumpolar distribution on Greenland, northern Russia, Siberia, northern Alaska, and the arctic coasts of Canada including most of the arctic islands, and perhaps the northern coast of Labrador. Winters on the north Pacific, especially along the Aleutian Islands, sometimes south as far as California; on the Atlantic coast from southern Greenland to Newfoundland, with occasional records to Georgia; and sometimes strays inland, especially on the Great Lakes.

Subspecies: None recognized.

IDENTIFICATION

In the Hand: Easily recognized as an eider on the basis of its sickle-shaped tertials and the extension of feathering along the sides and top of the bill, the king eider is the only eider (see also surf scoter) in which the feathering on the culmen extends farther forward than the lateral extension near the base of the bill. The unfeathered area between these two extensions is generally wider than in common eiders, particularly in males, where it is generally enlarged. Females are the only large eiders (folded wing 260-282 mm.) that exhibit crescent-shaped dark markings on the mantle and sides of the body.

In the Field: On the water, male king eiders show more black color than any of the other eiders, with the rear half of the body appearing black except for a narrow white line where the wings insert in the flanks and a white patch on the sides of the rump. The black "thorn feathers" among the rear scapulars protrude above the back conspicuously; in the common eider these either are not evident or are white (Pacific race). The enlarged reddish base of the bill is evident at great distances, even when the birds are in flight. Females are distinctly more reddish than female common eiders; they have crescentic body markings and a definite decumbent crest, which corresponds to the unique bluish feather area on the male. In flight, king eiders are slightly less bulky and ponderous than common eiders, and in a flock containing males the discontinuity of the white on their breasts and upper wing coverts caused by the black back color is plainly evident. Calls of the female king eider include loud *gog-gog-gog* notes, like the noise produced by a hammer hitting a hollow wooden wall, while males utter tremulous cooing sounds during their aquatic courtship.

NATURAL HISTORY

Habitat and Foods. The preferred breeding habitat of the king eider consists of freshwater ponds on arctic tundra, or lakes and streams not far from the coast. In a few cases they have been found nesting just above the high tide line of seacoasts, but more commonly they are found in the vicinity of fresh water. Outside the breeding season the birds are strictly limited to salt water, and they usually occur along coastlines or on the open ocean where the depths are shallow enough to permit easy diving for food. King eiders tend to forage farther from shore than do oldsquaws, scoters, or common eiders. They feed on foods similar to those of common eiders, with a predominance of bivalve mollusks, clams, and some echinoderms in their diet. Indeed, perhaps no other duck consumes such a variety or amount of echinoderms as does the king eider, with sand dollars and sea urchins being favored, but sea stars, brittle stars, and sea cucumbers also are taken at times.

Social Behavior. There is no certainty about when king eiders normally breed for the first time, but it seems likely that it occurs during the second or perhaps third year of life. Males in their second winter still

Breeding (hatched) and wintering (shaded) distributions of the king eider in North America.

retain some traces of immaturity, but do participate actively in social display. As with the common eider, inciting by the female seems to form a central feature of social display, and probably is the primary means by which individual associations between males and females are attained. The male displays have some similarities to those of common eiders, but the differing vocalizations and sharply different head and bill characteristics render the two species highly distinctive. Nevertheless, several wild hybrids between the two species have been observed, which indicates that the species are probably more closely related than their appearance would indicate. Precopulatory behavior of the two species is more similar than are the courtship displays, and ritualized bathing is especially frequent in this situation.

Reproductive Biology. During the egg-laying period, the male closely attends his mate and often follows her to the nest site for her egg-laying visits. Eggs are probably laid at the rate of one per day, in sites that are usually well dispersed and often on rather dry and rocky slopes at considerable distance from water. The average clutch size is about five eggs. Shortly after incubation begins the male deserts his mate and rapidly moves to the coast to begin a migration to favored molting areas that may be hundreds of miles from the breeding grounds. It is likely that the female spends very little time off her nest during the entire 22- to 24-day incubation period, since predation by jaegers, gulls, and other egg predators is probably very severe. Brood merging is extremely common in this species, and begins shortly after hatching. The number of females attending such "nurseries" varies, but up to a hundred or more young have been seen together, with as many as nine females in attendance. Apparently many of the females that are displaced from their broods flock together and migrate out of the area before molting, while the remaining females tend the young and remain with them through their entire fledging period, which is of uncertain length and may be as short as somewhat more than a month.

Conservation and Status. The king eider is certainly the most common of the North American eiders, although it is seen far less frequently than the common eider at lower latitudes. Much of the migration occurs past Point Barrow in extreme northern Alaska, where about a million eiders pass every fall, most of which are king eiders. In addition, another 100,000 or more king eiders occur in the eastern Canadian arctic and Greenland, so perhaps there are between 1 and 2 million king eiders in all of North America.

Suggested Reading. Johnsgard, 1975; Bellrose, 1976.

SPECTACLED EIDER
Somateria fischeri (Brandt) 1847
(Until 1973, regarded by the A.O.U. as *Lampronetta fischeri*)

Other Vernacular Names: None in general use.

Range: Breeds in eastern Siberia, and in North America along the west coast of Alaska, from Point Barrow or beyond south to St. Lawrence Island and the lower Kuskokwim River. Wintering area unknown, presumably in the north Pacific, but never observed in large numbers on the Aleutian Islands, where often presumed to winter.

Subspecies: None recognized.

IDENTIFICATION

In the Hand: Once determined to be an eider on the basis of its sickle-shaped tertials and partially feathered bill, spectacled eiders are easily recognized by the distinctive "spectacles" around the eyes or by the fact that the lateral surface of the bill from its base to a point above the nostrils is wholly feathered with short, velvety feathers. Females have brownish bodies with darker bars on the mantle and sides as in common eiders, but their smaller body size (maximum folded wing length 250 mm.) readily distinguishes them from that species if the head and bill characters cannot be examined.

In the Field: Male spectacled eiders are unmistakable in the field; the white eye-ring surrounded by green is visible for several hundred yards. Otherwise the top half of the bird appears white, while the bottom half is a dark silvery gray, including the lower breast. Females are generally tawny brown, with pale "spectacles" and a dark brown triangular area between the eye and the bill. Indeed, when females are crouching on nests these dark brown cheek markings are highly conspicuous and often reveal the female's presence. In flight, spectacled eiders fly with considerable agility, and the extension of the blackish underparts to a point well in front of the leading edge of the wings will serve to separate males from common eiders, while their white backs distinguish them from king eiders. Male spectacled eiders are unusually quiet, and their courtship calls are inaudible beyond about 20 yards. Female calls are very similar to those of the larger eiders.

NATURAL HISTORY

Habitat and Foods. Preferred breeding habitat of this species in western Alaska consists of rather luxuriant lowland tundra with small ponds and reasonable proximity to salt water. Small lakelets in coastal tundra are used for nesting in Siberia, and a few eiders nest as far as five to ten miles from the coastline in estuaries in Alaska. As soon as possible after the breeding season has been completed the eiders move back to sea; they are rarely seen through the fall, winter, and spring months. Summer food-analysis studies suggest that invertebrate life, especially mollusks, is the primary food, and birds collected during spring migration have been eating clams as a major part of their diet. Presumably the same kinds of foods are taken during winter, but there is no evidence on this, since the whereabouts of the flocks during that time of year remains a mystery.

Social Behavior. Since birds that are in their second winter have essentially attained an adult plumage pattern and participate in sexual display, it may be imagined that most pair bonds are formed initially in two-year-olds. Few observations of display have been made in the wild, but captive spectacled eiders sometimes begin display as early as the first week of January (in England), and it has been observed in wild birds in early June, shortly after arrival on the breeding grounds; thus, pair formation is probably a gradual process. The displays of both sexes are quite similar to those of common and king eiders; however, they are

Breeding (hatched) and presumptive wintering (shaded) distributions of the spectacled eider in North America.

performed somewhat more rapidly than in these larger species, and at least one of the display elements ("rearing") is almost identical to the major male display of the Steller eider. Behavior associated with copulation is much like that of the larger eiders, and includes the female remaining prone in the water while the male performs a series of bathing, preening, shaking, and similar displays derived from comfort movements.

Reproductive Biology. Spectacled eiders begin to spread out over the nesting habitat as soon as they arrive in spring, with most birds arriving already paired and the last stages of pair-forming behavior occurring in the others. Females seek out nest sites that usually are dead marsh grasses surrounding small tundra ponds, most often along the shore, on a small peninsula, or on an island. At least in some areas the nests seem to be slightly clustered, and have been observed as close as 12 feet apart, but in general there seems to be a tendency for coloniality. The average clutch consists of about four eggs, which are probably deposited one every other day. Once incubation begins, the female remains very attentive to her clutch, and during foraging intervals feeds predominantly on insect larvae, while immersing the head or tipping-up in shallow water. The young hatch in approximately 24 days, and there is no early movement of young to open water. Instead, the ducklings are reared to flight on fresh to slightly brackish water areas that are probably within a mile or two of the nest. At that time berries are eaten in quantity, as well as grasses, sedges, and some insect foods.

Conservation and Status. The lower Yukon, Kuskokwim delta region of Alaska is critical to the spectacled eider's survival, as it supports approximately 50,000 pairs in an average year, and sometimes up to 70,000, or at least a fourth of the total estimated world population of 200,000 birds. Of this total, about half or somewhat more are found in Alaska and the remainder nest in Siberia, mostly in the delta of the Indigirka River. Protection of these major breeding grounds is thus crucial to the long-term survival of this remarkable species.

Suggested Reading. Dau, 1974; Kistchinski and Flint, 1974.

STELLER EIDER
Polysticta stelleri (Pallas) 1769

Other Vernacular Names: None in general use.

Range: Breeds in arctic Siberia and in North America from at least St. Lawrence Island and the Kuskokwim Delta northward and eastward probably to Barter Island and Humphrey Point, with no definite nesting records for Canada. In North America, winters along the Aleutian Islands, Kodiak Island, and the Alaska Peninsula, rarely as far south as the Queen Charlotte Islands.

Subspecies: None recognized.

IDENTIFICATION

In the Hand: Quite different from the larger eiders, the Steller lacks feathering along the side and top of the bill, but does possess sickle-shaped tertials. Unlike those of any other species of diving duck, these tertials are iridescent blue on their outer webs, as are the secondaries. Other distinctive features are the narrow blackish bill, with soft marginal flaps near the tip, and a relatively long (up to 90 mm.), pointed tail.

In the Field: Because of their small size and agility, Steller eiders are more likely to be confused with dabbling ducks than with other eiders. The male's cinnamon-colored sides and breast are visible for long distances, as are the mostly white head and scapulars. The black markings around the eye and the rounded black spot between the breast and the sides are also unique. Females are best identified by their association with males. Their size and uniformly dark brown color are somewhat reminiscent of abnormally dark female mallards, and in flight they also exhibit a contrasting white underwing surface and two white wing bars. However, in taking off they run along the water like other diving ducks. The most conspicuous female call is a loud *qua-haaa'*, while males apparently produce only soft growling notes that are not audible over long distances.

NATURAL HISTORY

Habitat and Foods. The preferred breeding habitat of this small eider is lowland tundra closely adjacent to the coast. Tidewater flats having low eminences near a body of water are seemingly the primary nesting habitat. Rarely, nesting has been reported among dwarf birch and willow scrub, and in the Point Barrow area nests have been found on tundra some distance inland from the coast, but this is not believed to be the usual nesting habitat. The foods of Steller eiders are not well studied, and most of those that have been analyzed were collected during spring and summer months. At that time, crustaceans and mollusks apparently form the major part of the diet. Among samples obtained during winter there is also a predominance of crustaceans and mollusks. Generally, the birds seem to prefer to forage in shallow bays with muddy or sandy bottoms rather than along rocky shorelines, and apparently are adapted to feeding on soft-bodied organisms rather than heavy-shelled mollusks and crustaceans.

Social Behavior. It is probable that Steller eiders become reproductively mature in their second winter, although initial breeding may perhaps not occur until the third year. At least in captivity pair-forming behavior occurs over a period of several months, and in the wild it has been observed to occur at high intensity from late March through late April. As with the larger eiders, social display consists of many elements that represent ritualized comfort movements, including preening, shaking, bathing, and head-rolling, although wing-flapping does not occur

Breeding (hatched) and wintering (shaded) distributions of the
Steller eider in North America.

and the entire display repertoire is relatively silent. The most conspicuous display is called "rearing," and consists of a rapid upward and backward movement of the head and neck, exposing momentarily the chestnut-colored underparts. Females perform strong inciting movements with rather loud calling, and aerial chases are also frequent. Copulation is preceded by the female's assumption of a prone position and the male's performance of a series of alternating bill-dipping, bathing, and dorsal-preening movements.

Reproductive Biology. Relatively few observations have been made on nesting Steller eiders, but females evidently seek out nest sites in grassy cover that are often on the slight rise of a peninsula or along the edge of a tundra pond. The pair bond evidently remains intact until incubation is under way, or possibly even until about the time of hatching. The average clutch is seven eggs, and the nest is very thickly lined with dark brown down. The birds tend to nest slightly later than the other eiders and are very strong brooders, being extremely reluctant to leave their nests once incubation has begun. The incubation period is still unreported, but is likely to last about 24 days, based on what is known of the spectacled eider, and little is known about losses of eggs or ducklings to predators. Probably duckling mortality is fairly high, since well-grown broods seen in Alaska averaged only three to four young, suggesting an approximate 50 percent mortality rate. The fledging period is also unknown. There is a massive movement of adults out of the breeding areas before the molting season, and a premolt migration to Izembek Bay on the tip of the Alaska Peninsula, where birds from both Siberian and Alaskan breeding grounds undergo their flightless period.

Conservation and Status. The total world population of the Steller eider can barely be guessed at, but it certainly is concentrated in Siberia rather than in North America. The wintering population at Izembek Bay, Nelson Lagoon, and Becheven Bay, Alaska, probably represents nearly all of this total population, and in some years exceeds 200,000 birds. Since the primary nesting grounds of this species cannot be protected by American efforts, it is important that this important molting and wintering region be preserved and protected from disturbance. Suggested Reading. Brandt, 1943.

HARLEQUIN DUCK
Histrionicus histrionicus (Linnaeus) 1758

Other Vernacular Names: None in general use.

Range: Breeds in northern and eastern Asia, the islands of the Bering Sea and in continental North America and Alaska and the Yukon south through the western mountains to central California and Wyoming, and in northeastern North America from Baffin Island and Labrador to the Gaspé Peninsula and perhaps Newfoundland. Also breeds on Greenland and Iceland. Winters in North America from the Aleutian Islands south along the Pacific coast to California, and on the Atlantic coast from southern Canada to the New England states.

Subspecies: None recognized here. The supposed Pacific race *pacificus* is not acceptable (Dickinson, 1953; Todd, 1963).

IDENTIFICATION

In the Hand: Recognizable as a diving duck on the basis of its large feet with lobed hind toes and lengthened outer toes. The combination of an extremely short, narrow bill (culmen length 24-28 mm.) and moderately long wings (folded wing 190-210 mm.) that are at least slightly glossed with purplish on the secondaries will eliminate all other species. Males in nuptial plumage are unmistakable; no other duck is predominantly slate blue with white spots and stripes. Females and dull-colored males, however, are not so easily recognized, having facial markings similar to those of female surf and white-winged scoters, both of which are larger and have much heavier bills.

In the Field: Normally found only along rocky coastal shorelines or on timbered and rapid mountain streams, harlequins are small diving ducks that appear quite dark on the water. Both males and females have white to grayish white areas on the cheeks, white between the eye and the forehead (continuous with the white cheeks in males, usually separate in females), and a rounded white spot halfway behind the eyes and the back of the head. Males may have additional white spotting, especially as they acquire their nuptial plumage, but these facial areas remain white to grayish white in all plumages. In flight, both sexes appear relatively dark, both above and below, exhibiting dusky brown underwing coverts. When flying along mountain streams they remain quite low, following the course of the stream. When in coastal waters they forage in small flocks, often moving their heads in an elliptical fashion as they swim. Relatively silent birds, the male has a high-pitched, mouselike squeal, and females have a harsh croaking call.

NATURAL HISTORY

Habitat and Foods. The preferred breeding habitat of harlequin ducks appears to be cold, rapidly flowing streams that often but not always are surrounded by forests. The streams must be sufficiently well oxygenated to provide an adequate supply of suitable food in the form of aquatic insect larvae, and nest sites in rocky crevices or in dense vegetation that provides screening from above are also desirable. Outside the breeding season the birds are usually to be found in coastal situations where rock-bound bays and promontories occur. At this

Breeding (hatched) and wintering (shaded) distributions of the harlequin duck in North America.

time, mollusks such as chitons are extremely important foods, and crustaceans are also frequently eaten. During the breeding season a much higher proportion of insects is found in the diet, particularly of such types as midges, blackflies, caddis flies, and stone flies. Harlequins not only are adept in feeding in heavy surf, but also are extremely well adapted to foraging in torrential streams, where they feed by skimming the surface, immersing the head under water, and diving.

Social Behavior. Judging from the raising of captive birds, harlequin ducks attain their initial nuptial plumages the second winter of life, and at that age begin intensive sexual display. Partly because of the inaccessible habitats that these birds usually occupy, observations on their social displays are still incomplete, but an elliptical head-nodding is prevalent in both sexes and seems to function as an aggressive signal. Females evidently perform a kind of inciting display, but it seems to be infrequent and perhaps is not a central part of the pair-forming process. At least males and perhaps both sexes utter high-pitched screeching sounds during display, which otherwise tends to be rather silent. Before copulation the male performs several rather simple displays and makes short rushes toward the female, which gradually assumes a prone posture in the water.

Reproductive Biology. Harlequin ducks are noted for the extremely well concealed nest sites chosen by the females, which often nest on rather inaccessible islands; such sites typically are completely invisible from above. Tree-cavity nesting is apparently not as common as was once believed; the nest is usually on the ground and invariably is very close to water. The female may begin to incubate before the clutch has been completed, and typically begins to line the nest as incubation gets under way. The average clutch is probably only about six eggs, and the egg-laying interval is rather long, averaging about three days between eggs. The incubation period has not been firmly established, but probably lasts about 28 or 29 days, with some estimates of as long as 34 days. Males leave their mates once incubation begins, and begin to concentrate on favored foraging areas. Following hatching, the female takes her brood to a secluded part of the river, usually moving about very little. At times broods may merge, and be guarded by both females. Additionally, unsuccessful female breeders may sometimes also participate in brood care. The fledging period is still uncertain, but there is an early estimate of 40 days.

Conservation and Status. The distribution of this species is extremely localized, and nearly all of the North American population is concentrated along the Pacific coast. During fall and spring as many as a million harlequin ducks have been estimated to be present on the Aleutian Islands National Wildlife Refuge, which probably includes both North American and Asian breeding birds. Far fewer harlequin ducks are associated with the Atlantic coast of North America, and no specific population estimates are available.

Suggested Reading. Bengston, 1966, 1972, Kuchel, 1977.

OLDSQUAW
Clangula hyemalis (Linnaeus) 1758

Other Vernacular Names: Long-tailed Duck.

Range: Breeds in a circumpolar belt including arctic North America, Greenland, Iceland, northern Europe and Asia, and the islands of the Bering Sea. Winters in saltwater and deep freshwater habitats; in North America, from Alaska south to Washington and infrequently beyond on the Pacific coast, on the Great Lakes, and on the Atlantic coast south to South Carolina and rarely to Florida.

Subspecies: None recognized.

IDENTIFICATION

In the Hand: Probably the most seasonally variable in appearance of all North American waterfowl, oldsquaws may be recognized as diving ducks by their lobed hind toe and outer toe, and separated from other diving ducks by their short (culmen length 23-29 mm.) flattened bill with a raised nail, rather uniformly brownish upper wing coloration, and white or grayish sides and underparts. White is always present around the eye and may vary from a very narrow eye-ring to an extreme where almost the entire head is white.

In the Field: Found only on deep lakes, large rivers, or along the coast, oldsquaws are fairly small diving ducks at home in the heaviest surf or the most bitterly cold conditions. On the water the birds appear to be an almost random mixing of white, brown, and blackish markings, but invariably the flanks and sides are white, or no darker than light gray, and some white is present on the head, either around the eye or on the sides of the neck in both areas. Except during the summer molt, the elongated tail of males is also a good field mark, as are their black breasts. Lone females might be confused with female harlequin ducks, but they always have whitish rather than dark brown sides, and they may thus also be distinguished from immature or female scoters. In flight, oldsquaws exhibit white underparts that contrast with their dark upper and lower wing surfaces. The courtship calls of male oldsquaws are famous for their carrying power and rhythmic quality, the commonest two sounding like *ugh, ugh, ah-oo-gah'* and *a-oo, a-oo'-gah*.

NATURAL HISTORY

Habitat and Food. The primary breeding habitat of the oldsquaw throughout its entire range consists of arctic tundra in the vicinity of lakes, ponds, coastlines, or islands. Where shrubs are available for nesting cover they are preferentially utilized, but grasses and sedges are commonly used. Wooded country, however, is apparently avoided. Outside the breeding season the birds move to open water on large lakes, impoundments, and coasts. They are generally rather evenly distributed from open ocean and coastal bays through salt estuarine bays and brackish estuarine bays, becoming less abundant on freshwater estuaries. However, many also winter on the Great Lakes, especially those lakes providing abundant food in the form of small aquatic crustaceans and small bivalve mollusks. Some fish are also eaten, but these tend to be species of little or no commercial value. Nonetheless, oldsquaws are often caught in nets set out for whitefish, since both species tend to forage at the same depths and on the same amphipod crustaceans. Some birds have been drowned in nets set as deep as 150 feet, making them perhaps the deepest divers of all ducks.

Social Behavior. Oldsquaws attain their adult plumages in the second winter of life, and through much of the winter and spring months the birds engage in animated courtship displays. The displays tend to be highly aggressive, with much chasing on, below, and above the water surface, and are accompanied by loud calling on the part of the males. By comparison with male posturing, that of the females is slight, and mostly consists of a chin-lifting movement that is probably a form of inciting. As in the other sea ducks, copulation is usually preceded by the female assuming a prone position and the male performing an

Breeding (hatched) and wintering (shaded) distributions of the oldsquaw in North America.

extended series of displays, including bill-tossing, head-shaking, and other postures that seem to be but slightly modified from normal comfort movements.

Reproductive Biology. The arctic-nesting tendency of the oldsquaw allows but a bare minimum of time for breeding, and apparently the female hollows out her nest site immediately before laying the first egg. Nest sites are frequently on small islands, and usually are close to water. The egg-laying rate is approximately one per day, and normally six or seven eggs constitute a complete clutch. Females normally sit very tightly, but usually feed twice a day and on very warm days may leave the nest for several hours. The males abandon their mates about the time incubation begins, and either remain in the general area to undergo their molt or completely leave the area. The incubation period is 24 to 26 days, and after the ducklings hatch they are taken to freshwater ponds or lakes, or even at times may be led to salt water when only a few days old. As the birds grow older they gradually move from smaller sedge-lined lakelets to larger lakes and to marine waters. The fledging period is remarkably short, requiring only about five weeks, which is doubtless an adaptation to the very short frost-free period of the high arctic latitudes in which the birds frequently breed.

Conservation and Status. The extremely broad arctic nesting range of this species, its deep-water feeding adaptations, and its poor table qualities tend to place the oldsquaw out of direct contact with humans, and the worldwide population is probably among the highest of the sea ducks. It is impossible to make an accurate estimate of their numbers, which certainly must be in the millions. Summer populations in Alaska alone may be close to 600,000 birds, and the Canadian breeding range is far more extensive than that of Alaska.

Suggested Reading. Alison, 1975.

BLACK SCOTER
Melanitta nigra (Linnaeus) 1758
(Until 1973, regarded by the A.O.U. as *Oidemia nigra*)

Other Vernacular Names: American Scoter, Common Scoter, Coot.

Range: Breeds in Iceland, the British Isles, northern Europe, northern Asia, and islands of the Bering Sea; and in North America from northern Alaska probably across northern Canada, although specific breeding records are few and scattered. In North America, winters on the Pacific coast from the Pribilof and the Aleutian islands to southern California, on the Atlantic coast from Newfoundland south to about South Carolina, and to some extent in the interior, especially on the Great Lakes.

North American Subspecies:

M. m. nigra (L.): European Black Scoter. Breeds from Iceland eastward through Europe and Asia. Accidental in Greenland during winter.

M. m. americana (Swainson): American Black Scoter. Breeds and winters in North America as indicated above.

IDENTIFICATION

In the Hand: Recognizable in the hand as a diving duck by its enlarged hind toe and lengthened outer toe. The unusually narrow outermost primary (less evident in juveniles) and the relatively long (80-100 mm.), pointed tail will identify both sexes as black scoters. The bill is not feathered on the lateral surface or culmen, and no white feathers appear anywhere on the body except in juveniles, which have whitish underparts. The black is the smallest of the scoters, with a maximum folded wing length of 242 mm. in males and 230 mm. in females.

In the Field: Black scoter males are the blackest of all North American ducks, and females are the most uniformly dark brown of all these species. The best field mark for mature males, other than their black color, is a yellowish enlargement at the base of the bill, while females may be identified by the two-toned head and neck, which is dark brown above and grayish white on the cheeks, throat, and foreneck. Juveniles are similar, with an even sharper contrast to their head pattern. The birds take flight by running over the water, and they fly rather low but swiftly over the water. They appear dark brown or blackish on both the upper and the lower surfaces and have no white on the head or wings. The call of the courting male is a mellow whistle, while that of the female is grating and reminiscent of a door swinging on rusty hinges. The wings also produce a strong whistling noise in flight.

NATURAL HISTORY

Habitat and Foods. The breeding habitat of black scoters consists of freshwater ponds, lakes, or rivers in tundra or wooded country. Since shrubs are a favored type of scoter nest cover, it would seem that true lowland tundra probably does not represent ideal habitat, and instead the tundra–forest transition is most likely to provide such cover. Outside the breeding season black scoters are usually to be found at sea, where they forage in shallow areas that usually are within a mile of shore and are just beyond the breakers. There they both forage and rest, relatively independent of tidal action and free from human disturbance. This species seems to prefer areas where the water depth does not exceed 25 feet and where mussels can be found in large quantities. Other bivalves, such as rock clams, wedge clams, and razor clams, are also eaten in quantity, and barnacles, other crustaceans, and worms make up much of the remainder of their diet. Very little vegetable material is consumed by these birds.

Social Behavior. Although definite evidence is still lacking, it

Breeding (hatched) and wintering (shaded) distributions of the
black scoter in North America.

seems probable that at least some scoters breed at the end of their second year of life, and certainly birds in their second winter are in adult plumage. Social display occurs mostly at sea, and has been little studied in wild birds, but it apparently takes a form much like that of other sea ducks. It usually occurs in small flocks that typically contain a single female and five to eight males, with the number of males per group gradually increasing as the number of unmated females declines. Displays of the male consist of head-shaking, general shaking, and movements similar to normal comfort movements, but the most elaborate sequence consists of tail-cocking and a low rush over the water. Paired males perform many of the same displays toward their mates, but the relative frequency of these displays differs considerably from that of unpaired males.

Reproductive Biology. Black scoters are remarkably late arrivals at their breeding areas, which would seem to be a major disadvantage on their northernmost breeding grounds. In the Kuskokwim Delta of western Alaska they do not begin nesting until mid to late June, when many other species' ducklings are already hatching. The nests there are typically placed in the largest clumps of grass that can be found in the tundra, while in Iceland the birds much more commonly locate their nests under dense shrubbery, usually between 35 and 100 feet from the nearest water. There seems to be no special tendency to nest on islands. The average clutch consists of seven to nine eggs. Females are reputed to be very "tight" sitters, and are normally abandoned by their males shortly after incubation begins. Incubation lasts about 28 days. Little has been written of brood-rearing behavior, but apparently brood mergers, common in white-winged scoters, are not characteristic of this species. The fledging period is probably six to seven weeks. In some areas there is considerable migration out of the breeding grounds by males and nonbreeding females before the start of the molt.

Conservation and Status. The population dynamics of this species are extremely puzzling, since it is known to be a common nester in only very few areas of North America, primarily in western Alaska, and yet it is an abundant wintering bird on both coastlines. It is believed that Alaska may support about 235,000 black scoters, and that approximately that many winter in the Aleutian Islands alone. At minimum, there would seem to be at least a half million black scoters in North America, and more probably as many as a million.

Suggested Reading. Brandt, 1943.

SURF SCOTER
Melanitta perspicillata (Linnaeus) 1758

Other Vernacular Names: Coot, Skunk-head Coot.

Range: Breeds in North America from western Alaska eastward through the Yukon and the Northwest Territories to southern Hudson Bay, and in the interior of Quebec and Labrador. Winters on the Pacific coast from the Aleutian Islands south to the Gulf of California, and on the Atlantic coast from the Bay of Fundy south to Florida, with smaller numbers in the interior, especially on the Great Lakes.

Subspecies: None recognized.

IDENTIFICATION

In the Hand: Obviously a diving duck, on the basis of its enlarged hind toe and the outer toe as long or longer than the middle toe. Specimens can be verified as surf scoters if the outermost primary is longer than the adjacent one and feathering extends forward on the culmen almost to the rear edge of the nostrils. Additionally, there is a rounded or squarish black mark on the side of the bill near its base. Intermediate in size between the black and the white-winged scoters, surf scoters have a folded wing measurement of 240-256 mm. in males and 223-235 mm. in females.

In the Field: A maritime species that sometimes is found on large lakes or deep rivers during fall and winter, surf scoters may be distinguished on the water by the white markings on the male's forehead and nape, and the whitish cheek, ear, and nape markings of females. The white eye of adult males is often visible, but both sexes lack white on the wings. When landing, males frequently hold their wings upward and skid to a stop in the water, and when swimming, they usually hold the level of the bill slightly below horizontal. The male reportedly has a liquid, gurgling call uttered during courtship, and the female has a more crowlike note. In flight, the wings produce a humming sound, and the birds usually fly in irregular lines fairly low over the water.

NATURAL HISTORY

Habitat and Foods. The breeding habitat needs of this species have not been analyzed, since it has never received any special study on the nesting grounds. However, the birds probably are attracted to essentially the same habitats as attract the other scoters, namely freshwater ponds, lakes, or rivers, with shrubby cover of woodlands in the immediate vicinity. During the nonbreeding season they are found at sea or on large lakes. Similarly, the major food of surf scoters consists of mollusks, particularly blue mussels and related species. Altogether, bivalve mollusks constitute at least half of the species' food, although clams, scallops, and oysters are used relatively little. Evidently much of the foraging is done in early morning, when the birds feed beyond the breakers in depths of from 6 to 30 feet. They seem to feed in shallower waters and closer to shore than do the larger white-winged scoters.

Social Behavior. Surf scoters presumably mature in their second winter of life, when their plumage reaches the adult condition. During late winter and spring a good deal of social display occurs, most of it in separate small groups of birds consisting of a single female and several males. A good deal of ritualized threatening behavior is evident in these groups, with the males often attacking one another and the female threatening any male that approaches too closely. The male postures and movements are several, and one of the most conspicuous is "breast-scooping," which seems to be a ritualized form of breast preening and is accompanied by a liquid, gurgling call. Short display flights are also common, and as the male lands he holds his wings in an upward V posture as he skids to a stop in the water. The most elaborate ritualized display is probably "chest-lifting," a sudden rearing backward in the

Breeding (hatched) and wintering (shaded) distributions of the surf scoter in North America.

water that bears an uncanny resemblance to the rearing display of the Steller eider and spectacled eider. Before copulation, the female assumes a prone posture and remains motionless in it, sometimes for as long as several minutes. The male then performs bill-dipping, ritualized drinking, and preening movements, in no obvious sequence. Following treading the male performs a single chest-lifting display, which is likewise comparable to the postcopulatory display of the Steller eider.

Reproductive Biology. Extremely little has been written on the reproduction of surf scoters. The few available observations indicate that the nests are well scattered over wide areas, and usually are placed some distance from the water. They tend to be very well concealed, often under the low-spreading branches of pine or spruce trees. However, these birds have also been reported to nest close to water in Labrador, placing their nests in grass or under bushes. The clutch probably normally consists of five to seven eggs, but neither the incubation nor the fledging periods have been determined.

Conservation and Status. As with other scoters, population estimates of this species must be based on a good deal of guesswork, since the three species of scoters are often collectively counted during aerial surveys. This species is generally the commonest of the three on wintering areas, and it has been suggested that as many as about 750,000 surf scoters breed in Alaska alone. Probably the Canadian breeding population is substantially larger than the Alaskan one, so perhaps as many as 2 or 3 million surf scoters breed in North America. This is an almost unbelievable figure, given the fact that so very few surf scoter nests have ever been located.

Suggested Reading. Johnsgard, 1975; Bellrose, 1976.

WHITE-WINGED SCOTER
Melanitta fusca (Linnaeus) 1758
(Melanitta deglandi of A.O.U., 1957)

Other Vernacular Names: Velvet Scoter, White-winged Coot.

Range: Breeds in Scandinavia, Estonia, northern Russia, and north-eastern Siberia; and in North America from northwestern Alaska, the Yukon, the Northwest Territories east to Hudson Bay, and south through western Canada to southern Manitoba and rarely to north-central North Dakota. Winters on both coasts of North America, from Alaska to Baja California and from the Gulf of St. Lawrence to South Carolina.

North American Subspecies:

  M. f. deglandi (Bonaparte): American White-winged Scoter. Breeds in North America as indicated above. Delacour (1959) rejects the validity of the Pacific coastal race *dixoni*.

  M. f. fusca (L.): European White-winged (Velvet) Scoter. Breeds in Europe and Asia; in North America occurs casually in Greenland.

IDENTIFICATION

In the Hand: As in other diving ducks, the enlarged hind toe and lengthened outer toe are present, and specimens may be recognized as a scoter by the heavy bill and rather uniformly dark body. Unlike the other scoters, it has a bill that is feathered laterally to a point near the posterior edge of the nostrils, its outermost primary is shorter but not appreciably narrower than the adjoining one, and its speculum is white. The white-winged is the largest of the scoters, with folded wing measuring from 269 to 293 mm. in males and from 251 to 266 mm. in females.

In the Field: White-winged scoters are usually found on the coast but are more likely than the other scoters to be found on large interior lakes during winter. On the water the white wing markings are sometimes not visible, and a white eye-patch on the male may be the only apparent part of the bird that is not dark brown or black. Adult females very closely resemble female surf scoters on the water, but never exhibit whitish nape markings. The blackish crown of the former contrasts less sharply with the sides of the head, and the pale cheek and ear markings are generally less apparent than in the latter. As soon as the birds flap their wings or fly, the white secondary markings become apparent and provide the best field marks. In flight, white-winged scoters are the most ponderous of the scoters, usually flying low over the water in loose flocks or long lines. Males possess a bell-like, repeated whistled note, and females are said to also utter a very thin whistle.

NATURAL HISTORY

Habitat and Foods. Although the habitat needs of the North American race of white-winged scoter have not been analyzed, those of the European race are well studied. There, nesting on open tundra is rare, and the coastal archipelagos and lakes of the northern coniferous forest zone seem to represent the original breeding habitat. Coastal areas having boulder-strewn islets that are dominated by herbaceous vegetation but with shrubs and trees also present seem to represent the ideal habitat. The species is also attracted to nesting among gull or tern colonies. During the rest of the year white-winged scoters are usually to be found at sea, often within a mile from shore but just beyond the zone of breakers. In estuaries they are likely to be found in saltwater areas rather than brackish or slightly brackish habitats. Bivalve mollusks are the favorite food of white-winged scoters, with rock clams, oysters, and mussels all consumed in large quantities. Crustaceans are also eaten, as well as smaller quantities of insects, fishes, and some plant foods.

Social Behavior. Pair bonds are renewed each year among sexually mature birds, and it is believed that maturity is attained in the second

Breeding (hatched) and wintering (shaded) distributions of the
white-winged scoter in North America.

winter of life. The white-winged scoter's social behavior and sexual displays are much like those of the other scoters, and include a considerable number of movements not obviously modified from the corresponding comfort movements of the species. Actual or ritualized threats are common among the males, and attacks are also frequent. Additionally, several displays observed in courting groups also serve as precopulatory displays of males, as is the case also with eiders. These include a ritualized or "false" drinking display, preening movements, and "water-twitching" with the bill immersed. Females have a chin-lifting display that probably serves as an inciting posture, and frequently they also make short attacks toward the males.

Reproductive Biology. White-winged scoters usually arrive rather late on their breeding grounds, but despite this they do not exhibit a rapid transition to nesting behavior. Sometimes nearly a month elapses between spring arrival and the start of egg-laying. The nest site is apparently chosen with care, as it is almost always extremely well concealed, and frequently is placed in a natural cavity or under a rock overhang that provides concealment from above. The shoreline zone seems to be avoided for nesting, and instead wooded areas sometimes rather far from shore seem to be preferred. A clutch of about nine eggs is typical, with the eggs being laid at average intervals of about forty hours. Males abandon their mates at about the beginning of incubation. Incubation lasts 26 to 29 days. After hatching, females take their broods to relatively open brood-rearing habitats, where brood merging is often frequent. In this way, aggregations of up to 100 or more young may develop, and are tended by a number of females.

Conservation and Status. As in the other scoters, it is difficult to reconcile the apparent scarcity of this species on breeding areas with its abundance on the wintering grounds. It has been suggested that the breeding population of the white-winged scoters in North America may be about 675,000 birds, but most of the scoters nesting in western Canada are believed to be of this species, and thus this figure seems conservative.

Suggested Reading. Koskimies and Routamo, 1953.

BUFFLEHEAD
Bucephala albeola (Linnaeus) 1758

Other Vernacular Names: Butterball.

Range: Breeds from southern Alaska and northern Mackenzie District through the forested portions of Canada east to James Bay and south into the western United States to northern California and Wyoming. Winters along the Pacific coast from the Aleutian Islands to central Mexico, along the Gulf and Atlantic coasts from Texas to southern Canada, and in the interior where open water occurs.

Subspecies: None recognized.

IDENTIFICATION

In the Hand: The smallest of all the North American diving ducks, this is the only species that has a lobed hind toe, an adult folded wing measurement of 180 mm. or less, and a tail of less than 80 mm. The very short (culmen length 23-29 mm.), narrow bill is also distinctive, and there is always some white present behind the eye.

In the Field: In spite of their small size, male buffleheads in nuptial plumage can be seen for great distances; their predominantly white plumage sets them apart from all other small ducks except the extremely rare smew. The disproportionately large head with its white crest is also apparent, especially when the crest is maximally spread. The tiny female is much less conspicuous and is usually only seen after sighting the male, when its small size and white teardrop or oval marking behind the eye provide identifying field marks. In flight, buffleheads are more agile than most other diving ducks, and their small wings, which are dusky below, beat rapidly and flash the white speculum and upper wing covert coloration. Both sexes are relatively silent, even during courtship display. They are likely to be confused only with hooded mergansers when in flight, but the shorter, rounded head as well as the shorter bill set them apart from this species quite easily.

NATURAL HISTORY

Habitat and Foods. During the breeding season the favored habitat of buffleheads consists of ponds and lakes in or near open woodlands. The presence of suitable nest cavities, often old woodpecker holes, no doubt contributes substantially to the suitability of an area for nesting. An availability of summer foods in the form of insects, such as water boatmen, aquatic beetles, and their larvae, also may be of special importance. Alkaline ponds, sloughs, and small lakes, which are often rich in invertebrate life, are favored over large lakes and high mountain ponds, and trees having suitable nesting cavities should be either surrounded by water or very close to its shore. Fairly open shorelines with only sparse reedbeds are also favored. Buffleheads are found on freshwater as well as marine habitats outside the breeding season. In freshwater areas they tend to concentrate on insects and mollusks. In saltwater environments insects are largely replaced by crustaceans as primary foods, while mollusks also remain important. Generally the birds seem to prefer to forage in water from 4 to 15 feet deep, and tend to inhabit larger and relatively open bodies of water.

Social Behavior. Buffleheads mature in their second winter of life, and at least some two-year-old females attempt to nest. Social display occurs over a several-month period during winter and spring, and is a highly animated and complex activity, with many ritualized patterns of display. Inciting by the female forms the focus of display, and male display seems to be largely derived from aggressive tendencies. Actual attacks, both above and below the water, are also frequent, as are short display flights by the males. Crest-raising is perhaps the most obvious

Breeding (hatched) and wintering (shaded) distributions of the bufflehead in North America.

male display, but a pumping movement of the head is especially frequent as well. Before copulation, the female assumes a prone posture and remains in it while the male performs such displays as preening and dipping and shaking the bill while in water. In these displays the bufflehead exhibits its close evolutionary relationships both to the other goldeneyes and to the scoters.

Reproductive Biology. Shortly after arriving on their nesting grounds, female buffleheads begin to seek out suitable nest sites. There is a strong tendency for females to return to the area in which they were raised, and many times they will nest in exactly the same nest site if it is available. Cavities with holes barely large enough to admit the female seem to be preferred, and these include old woodpecker holes that are less than three inches in diameter. The female is a notoriously "tight" sitter, and lays a clutch that averages nine eggs, with the eggs being laid at approximately 40-hour intervals. The incubation period is about 30 days, and during that period the male abandons his mate and typically leaves the nesting area. Following hatching the female usually broods her young for 24 to 36 hours before leaving the nest. After the brood has jumped from the nest to land, they move to the nearest water area. The fledging period of the young is about 50 to 55 days.

Conservation and Status. The bufflehead is certainly one of the most attractive of all North American waterfowl, and its status has been generally favorable. It has been estimated that its average breeding-season population may be about 500,000 birds, but there are large annual fluctuations in survey data. At present no clear-cut trends are evident, although the species seems to be declining in the western part of its range while it is increasing in the easternmost areas.

Suggested Reading. Erskine, 1972.

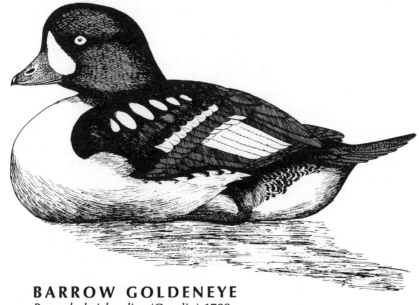

BARROW GOLDENEYE
Bucephala islandica (Gmelin) 1789

Other Vernacular Names: Whistler.

Range: Breeds in Iceland, southwestern Greenland, northern Labrador, and from southern Alaska and Mackenzie District southward through the western states and provinces to California and Wyoming. Winters primarily along the Pacific coast from Alaska to central California, and on the Atlantic coast from southern Canada to the mid-Atlantic states.

Subspecies: None recognized.

IDENTIFICATION

In the Hand: The presence of white markings on the middle secondaries and their adjoining coverts, yellow feet with a lobed hind toe, and yellowish eyes will serve to separate this species from all others except the common goldeneye. Adult male Barrow goldeneyes are very much like male common goldeneyes, but differ in the following characteristics: (1) The head iridescence is glossy purple, and the white cheek marking is crescentic in shape; (2) the head has a fairly flat crown, and the nail is distinctly raised above the contour of the gradually taper-ing bill; and (3) the body is more extensively black, especially on the flanks, which are heavily margined (at least ⅔ inch) with black, and on the scapulars, which are margined with black on an elongated outer web or both webs, producing a pattern of oval white spots separated by a black background. The upper wing surface is also more extensively black, with the exposed bases of the greater secondary coverts black and the marginal, the lesser, and most of the middle coverts also blackish. Only about five secondaries have their exposed webs entirely white, while the more distal ones may be white-tipped. The length of the bill's nail is at least 12 mm. in this species, as compared with a maximum of 11 mm. in the common goldeneye (Brooks, 1920).

Females are closely similar to female common goldeneyes, but may be separable by (1) the somewhat darker brown head, which is relatively flat-crowned in shape; (2) the brighter and more extensively yellow bill during the spring, especially in western populations, where it is usually entirely yellow; (3) the sooty middle and lesser wing coverts, which are only narrowly tipped with grayish white; and (4) the broader and more pronounced ashy brown breast band. Brooks (1920) reported that the shape of the bill and the length of the nail provide the best criteria, with the common goldeneye having a nail length that never exceeds 10 mm. (average 9.4) and the Barrow goldeneye having a nail length greater than 10 mm. (average 10.9).

In the Field: A lone female can be separated from common golden-eye females in the field only by the most experienced observers, but its somewhat darker head with its flatter crown is usually apparent, and any female with a completely yellow bill is most likely to be a Barrow goldeneye, although Brooks (1920) noted one possible exception to this rule. A male in nuptial plumage appears to be predominantly black in the upperparts to a point below the insertion of the wing, with a row of neatly spaced white spots extending from the midback forward to-ward the breast, where an extension of black continues down in front of the "shoulder" to the sides of the breast. Its head is distinctly "flat-topped," with a long nape and a purplish head gloss, and there is a crescentic white mark in front of the eye. In flight, females of the two goldeneyes appear almost identical (the yellow bill is often quite ap-parent in the Barrow during spring), but the white marking on the upper wing surface of the male is interrupted by a black line on the greater secondary coverts. Male Barrow goldeneyes have no loud whistled notes during courtship; the commonest sounds are clicking noises and soft grunting notes. Head-pumping movements of the female are of a rotary rather than elliptical form, and lateral head-turning or inciting movements are much more frequent in the Barrow goldeneye. As in the common goldeneye, a whistling noise is produced by the wings during flight.

NATURAL HISTORY

Habitat and Foods. The breeding habitat of this species consists of lakes or ponds, often in the vicinity of wooded country. Where trees having large natural cavities are absent, rock crevices may serve for nest sites. Additionally, a local abundance of food in the form of aquatic invertebrates plays an important part in determining nesting distribution. These birds are often found in somewhat alkaline lakes which are fairly deep and tend to lack much shoreline vegetation. Typical wintering habitats include both freshwater and brackish areas, rather than saltwater environments. Most of the food consumed through the year is of animal origin, with insects, mollusks, and crustaceans making up the majority. In some areas salmon eggs are seasonally important, but plant materials are always in the minority.

Social Behavior. Barrow goldeneyes mature in the second winter of life, and from that point onward spend a great deal of time in social display during winter and spring months. Inciting by the female serves as the primary stimulus for male displays, which are highly ritualized modifications of aggressive tendencies. Additionally, actual threats and attacks are common, as are chases, both above and below water. The displays of male Barrow goldeneyes are much like those of the common goldeneye, but are slightly less diverse; only a single type of head-throw posture is present, in contrast to the three types found in the common goldeneye. The vocalizations are also distinctly different, and presumably some of these differences tend to prevent hybridization between the two species, which has been reported only a few times for wild birds. In both species the behavior associated with copulation is extremely prolonged, and consists mostly of drinking, stretching, and similar behavior that closely resembles the normal comfort movements of the birds.

Reproductive Biology. After the birds have returned to their nesting areas, females begin to search for suitable nest cavities. In Iceland,

Breeding (hatched) and wintering (shaded) distributions of the
Barrow goldeneye in North America.

where trees are nearly absent, most nests are in holes or cavities in the ground, while most of the rest are well hidden under shrubs. In British Columbia, however, cavities in live trees, tree stumps, or tall dead stumps are the usual sites. Tree cavities with vertical entrances are used rather frequently, and most have entrances between 3 and 4 inches in diameter. The average clutch is of nine eggs, but competition for nest sites sometimes inflates this number through the addition of eggs laid by more than one female. Incubation requires an average of about 32 days. After hatching, the female establishes a brood territory, from which other goldeneye females and broods are forcibly excluded, and sometimes even the young of other species are attacked. Females typically abandon their brood when the young are well grown but are still unfledged. Fledging reportedly requires about eight weeks, and thereafter the young birds gradually move toward their wintering areas.

Conservation and Status. The North American population of this species is divided into two segments, a very small eastern component and a very large western one. Good population figures are not available for either of these, but it has been suggested that from 125,000 to 150,000 birds may be present in the spring in British Columbia and Alaska, the principal breeding range. South of Canada there may be a few thousand additional pairs, mostly in Washington and Montana. The species is not hunted preferentially, and is unlikely to provide a serious conservation problem in the foreseeable future.

Suggested Reading. Munro, 1939.

COMMON GOLDENEYE
Bucephala clangula (Linnaeus) 1758

Other Vernacular Names: Golden-eye Duck, Whistler.

Range: Breeds in Iceland, northern Europe and Asia from Norway to Kamchatka, and in North America from Alaska to southern Labrador and Newfoundland, and southward through the forested portions of the northern and northeastern United States. Winters in North America from the southern Alaska coast south through the western states to California, the interior states wherever open water is present, and the Atlantic coast from Florida to Newfoundland.

North American Subspecies:

B. c. *americana* (Bonaparte) : American Common Goldeneye. Breeds in North America as indicated above.

IDENTIFICATION

In the Hand: Males in nuptial plumage or those in their first spring of life have a characteristic oval white mark between the yellowish eye and the bill. Mature males, even when in eclipse plumage, are the only North American ducks that have the combination of a folded wing length of at least 215 mm. and an uninterrupted white wing patch extending from the middle secondaries forward over the adjoining greater, middle, and lesser coverts. Females can be distinguished from all other species except the Barrow goldeneye by their lobed hind toe, a folded wing length of 190 mm. or more, the white on the middle secondaries, and their greater coverts (which are tipped with dusky) and at least the adjoining middle coverts more grayish or whitish than the tertials or lesser coverts. See the Barrow goldeneye account for characteristics that will serve to separate females of these two species.

In the Field: Along with the larger and more streamlined common merganser, goldeneyes are the only large diving ducks that appear to be mostly white-bodied, with blackish backs and heads. The oval white mark on the male can be seen for considerable distances, and even if this mark is not definitely visible, the common goldeneye male differs from the Barrow goldeneye male in several other apparent ways. The former's head is more triangular in shape, with the top almost pointed rather than flattened, the nape is not extended into a long crest, and a greenish gloss is apparent in good light. The upper half of the body appears predominantly white, with parallel black lines extending diagonally backward above the folded wing, and no black is evident on the side of the breast. In flight, both species of goldeneye exhibit dusky underwing coverts, but the common goldeneye exhibits a relatively continuous white upper wing patch, at least in males. The male's calls are varied, but the loudest and most conspicuous is a shrill *zeee-at* note that is associated with aquatic head-throw displays. Females of both species are relatively silent. The wings of males produce a strong whistling noise during flight.

NATURAL HISTORY

Habitat and Foods. The preferred habitat of the common goldeneye consists of permanent water areas having marshy shores and adjacent stands of large hardwood trees that provide nest sites. Both moving-water and standing-water habitats seem to be equally acceptable, and the depth of the water apparently is also not important, but it must provide adequate food in the form of aquatic invertebrate life. Many aquatic insects are eaten, as is a variety of crustaceans, and mollusks represent the third important food source. The birds seem to be relatively opportunistic, feeding on whatever is locally available, and they generally forage in waters between 4 and 20 feet deep. During the win-

Breeding (hatched) and wintering (shaded) distributions of the common goldeneye in North America.

ter the birds are found in a wide variety of habitats, ranging from fresh-water to marine, and from rivers to large impoundments.

Social Behavior. Goldeneyes become sexually mature and begin to pair in their second winter of life, and perhaps to a greater degree than almost any other species of diving duck seem to devote a remarkably large portion of their time to social display. This occurs from late fall through the winter and spring migration, and some display even seems to occur among paired birds. The female displays are simple, and mainly consist of ritualized inciting movements, plus a distinctive neck-dipping movement that seems to be a particularly strong stimulus for display by males. An astonishing variety of male displays is present, and they are notable not only for their number but also for their stereotypy of form and timing. Many are obviously derived from hostile behavior, but others are of no clear origin. Among them are a head-throw display and a fast and a slow form of head-throw-kick. Copulation is preceded by the female assuming a prone posture and remaining motionless while the male performs a long and seemingly unprogrammed series of displays derived from preening, bathing, stretching, and similar comfort movements. Only the displays that immediately precede treading have a specific form and sequence, and this sequence is very similar to that of the Barrow goldeneye.

Reproductive Biology. Goldeneyes are relatively early migrants, and females begin to seek out suitable nesting cavities soon after their arrival in breeding areas. Favored nest sites are in hardwood trees having cavities with lateral openings, but the size of the entrance and the height of the cavity seems to matter but little. Favored trees are those in open stands near the edges of marshes or fields, and those which have cavity diameters of about 6 to 10 inches. A clutch of about nine eggs is typical, with the eggs laid at average intervals of about two eggs every three days. In some areas competition for limited nest sites results in abnormally large clutches as a result of multiple use of cavities. Additionally, female common mergansers sometimes compete for the same site, which usually results in desertion by the goldeneye. Incubation requires 27 to 32 days, probably averaging about 30. Normally on the morning following hatching the female calls the young from the nest, and they typically jump out in rapid succession. After the entire brood has left the nest the family begins to walk toward the nearest water, which may be a mile or more away. Female goldeneyes seem much more inclined to lose or abandon part of their brood than are most other ducks, and thus many young birds are forced to try to survive on their own. The fledging period is approximately eight to nine weeks, and as the birds fledge they begin to group with other juveniles and move toward wintering areas.

Conservation and Status. There is no good information on this species' population status in North America, but a rough estimate of 1.25 million birds in the breeding season has been made. Because of the bird's high adaptability in foraging and wintering habitats, it seems unlikely that the common goldeneye will pose any conservation problems so long as suitable forested breeding areas remain.

Suggested Reading. Carter, 1958.

HOODED MERGANSER
Mergus cucullatus (Linnaeus) 1758
(Lophodytes cucullatus of A.O.U., 1957)

Other Vernacular Names: Fish Duck, Hairyhead, Sawbill.

Range: Breeds from southeastern Alaska and adjacent Canada eastward through the southern and middle wooded portions of the border provinces to New Brunswick and Nova Scotia; southward to Oregon and Idaho, in a southeasterly direction across the wooded parts of the northern Great Plains to the Mississippi Valley, and from there to the Atlantic coast and sporadically as far south as the Gulf coast states. Winters along the Pacific coast from southern British Columbia south to Mexico, along the Gulf coast, along the Atlantic coast north to the New England states, and to some extent in the interior, especially on the Great Lakes.

Subspecies: None recognized.

IDENTIFICATION

In the Hand: Apart from the very rare smew, this is the only species with a merganserlike bill (narrow, serrated, with a large, curved nail), a culmen length less than 45 mm., and a folded wing measurement less than 205 mm. Additionally, the rounded crest, yellowish legs, and ornamental black or brownish tertials with narrow white or ashy stripes are all distinctive.

In the Field: On the water, both sexes appear as small ducks with long, thin bills and fanlike crests that are usually only partially opened. Only the bufflehead has a comparable white crest, and that species lacks reddish brown flanks, has no black margin on the crest, and has a much shorter bill. Immature males or females appear as slim grayish brown birds with a brownish head and a cinnamon-tinted crest. In flight, hooded mergansers lower the crest and hold the head at the same level as the body, making a streamlined profile, and exhibit their distinctive black and white upper wing pattern, while their underwing coloration is mostly silvery gray and whitish. Females are not highly vocal, but during courtship activities the distinctive male call, a rolling, frog-like *crrrooooo,* may be heard for some distance.

NATURAL HISTORY

Habitat and Foods. The preferred habitat of the hooded merganser consists of wooded, clear-water streams and, to a lesser degree, wooded shorelines of lakes. The combination of food in the form of small fish and invertebrates in water sufficiently clear for foraging and suitable nest sites in the form of tree cavities is probably a major factor influencing this species' breeding distribution. Like the wood duck, the hooded merganser seems rather sensitive to cold, and its breeding range does not extend as far north as the northern limit of forested habitat. The foods of the hooded merganser include fish, insects, frogs, tadpoles, snails, other mollusks, crayfish, and other small crustaceans. The birds prefer to feed in clear water having sandy or cobble bottoms, and also in relatively shallow streams.

Social Behavior. Hooded mergansers probably become sexually mature in their second winter, although it has been observed that some yearling males display and may form loose pair bonds. The displays of the hooded merganser are of special interest, since they share many char-

Breeding (hatched) and wintering (shaded) distributions of the
hooded merganser in North America.

acteristics with the displays of goldeneyes, and provide evidence that these two rather different-looking groups of birds are actually closely related, an idea that is supported by the occasional occurrence of wild common goldeneye-hooded merganser hybrids. Courting groups usually consist of one or two females and several males; as might be expected, crest-raising and other displays involving the exhibition of the crest are very well developed. A head-throw display is present and is accompanied by a rather rolling and froglike call, and silent head-pumping movements similar to those of goldeneyes are also common. Females perform inciting, and also have a head-pumping movement similar to that of the males. Copulation is preceded by the assumption of a prone position on the part of the female, and a series of male displays given in a sequence similar to that typical of goldeneyes and having several elements in common with them.

Reproductive Biology. Probably a good deal of time is required for females to locate suitable nest sites, which are always in cavities and usually in tree hollows. Artificial nest boxes are sometimes used by these birds, and they seem to use such boxes when they are placed in open impoundments rather than those where dead timber is present. Boxes placed close to water are also more frequently used than those some distance from it. The birds are very similar in size to wood ducks, and readily accept nest boxes made for that species. After locating a nest cavity, females begin to lay eggs at the rate of one every other day. Down is usually not deposited until the clutch, which consists of about ten eggs, has been completed. The incubation period is about 32 or 33 days, rather surprisingly long for such a small bird. After the young have hatched they are taken by the female to brood-rearing areas, which usually are shallow, wide, and sandy or cobble-bottomed streams high in invertebrate life and small fish. The fledging period is about ten weeks, but it is not known exactly when the female usually abandons her brood to begin her own postnuptial molt.

Conservation and Status. Regrettably little can be said with confidence about the population of this unique and beautiful species. One recent calculation by Frank Bellrose placed the probable spring population at about 76,000 birds. However, we have no idea as to whether the population is increasing or declining, or at what rate. If, like the other mergansers, it has suffered from unjustified mistreatment at the hands of hunters and from poisoning by ingestion of pesticides, its status should be much more closely monitored than it is at present.

Suggested Reading. Morse *et al.*, 1969.

SMEW
Mergus albellus (Linnaeus) 1758

Other Vernacular Names: None in North America.
Range: Breeds in northern Europe and Asia from Scandinavia to Kamchatka and Anadyr. Winters in southern Europe and Asia south to the Indian Ocean; accidental in North America.
Subspecies: None recognized.

IDENTIFICATION

In the Hand: This rare Eurasian merganser is best identified in the hand, where it can be recognized as a merganser by its narrow, tapering bill with serrated edges and a prominent nail. It is the only merganser with a short bill (culmen length 25-30 mm.), white upperwing coverts, and grayish legs.
In the Field: The predominantly white male is not much larger than a bufflehead, but the smew's head is mostly white, rather than blackish, and has a narrow black stripe behind the eyes instead of a large white patch behind the eyes. Otherwise, the body patterns of the two

species are quite similar, but the bufflehead lacks the two black stripes extending from the foreback down the sides of the breast. Females cannot safely be identified by persons lacking experience with the species, but apart from the merganserlike bill, they have a sharply bicolored head, with a chocolate brown cap extending through the eyes, and with white cheeks, throat, and foreneck. The rest of the body is a rather uniform gray. In flight, both sexes exhibit a great deal of white on the inner half of the upper wing surface, with two black stripes toward the rear of the wing. Like other mergansers, they fly with the neck and head held at the same level as the body.

RED-BREASTED MERGANSER
Mergus serrator Linnaeus 1758

Other Vernacular Names: Fish Duck, Saw-bill.

Range: Breeds in Greenland, Iceland, the British Isles, northern Europe and Asia from Scandinavia to Kamchatka, the Aleutian Islands, and from Alaska eastward across nearly all of arctic Canada except the northern part of Keewatin District and the arctic islands, south to northern British Columbia and Alberta, central Saskatchewan and Manitoba, southern Ontario, the Great Lakes states, northern New York, New England, and the eastern provinces of Canada to Newfoundland. Winters mostly on salt water, in North America from southeastern Alaska south to Baja California, the Gulf coast, the Atlantic coast from Florida to the Gulf of St. Lawrence, and inland in smaller numbers as far north as the Great Lakes.

North American subspecies:

    M. s. serrator L.: Common Red-breasted Merganser. Breeds as indicated above, except in Greenland.

    M. s. schiøleri Salomonsen: Greenland Red-breasted Merganser. Resident in Greenland.

IDENTIFICATION

In the Hand: The long, narrow, serrated bill with a hooked tip will distinguish this species from all other mergansers except the common merganser. In the red-breasted merganser the bill is distinctive in that (1) the nostrils are located in the basal third of the bill, (2) the feathering on the side of the upper mandible reaches considerably farther forward than that on the lower mandible, (3) the upper mandible is relatively longer and lower at the base than in other mergansers, at least six or more times as long as it is high at the base when measured from the cutting edge to the highest unfeathered point, and (4) the bill has a smaller, narrower nail at the tip. Both sexes are smaller than the common merganser, with adult males and females having maximum folded wing lengths of 260 and 230 mm., respectively.

In the Field: When in nuptial plumage, the male red-breasted merganser may be recognized by its green head, which extends backward into a shaggy double crest and is separated in front from a brownish breast by a white foreneck. The sides and flanks appear to be a light gray, bordered anteriorly with a black patch having regular white spots. The female is not nearly so "two-toned" as the female common merganser; her grayish body merges gradually with the brownish head, and neither the paler throat nor the lores are in strong contrast to the rest of the head. The female calls of the two species are very similar, but the courtship notes of the male red-breasted merganser are a somewhat catlike *yeow-yeow*, uttered during bizarre posturing. In flight, both sexes resemble the common merganser, but males exhibit a brownish breast band, while females appear to have a darker brown, less reddish head and neck color, which gradually merges with the grayish breast.

NATURAL HISTORY

Habitat and Foods. The favored breeding habitat of this species would appear to be inland freshwater lakes and streams not far from the coast. Deep, rock-lined lakes are apparently favored over tundra pools, but the ground-nesting adaptations of this species allow it to nest in nonforested situations well away from a source of hollow trees. Boulder-strewn areas are rich in potential nest sites and thus are especially favored. In contrast to the freshwater tendencies of the hooded merganser and common merganser, this species is usually found in

Breeding (hatched) and wintering (shaded) distributions of the
red-breasted merganser in North America.

saline environments outside the breeding season, and sometimes occurs on the open ocean as well as in most estuarine habitats. It feeds almost exclusively on fish throughout the year, but these tend to be small and easily captured species. It also feeds on salmon eggs, but these are primarily opaque salmon eggs, which are considered largely a waste product. In the most complete study to date, it was found that commercial game fish constituted only 14 percent of the foods found in an analysis of 130 stomachs.

Social Behavior. Red-breasted mergansers become sexually active in the second winter of life, when they attain adult plumage for the first time. Social display occurs during the winter and spring months, and much of it takes place while the birds are on salt water. The calls and posturing are surprisingly different from those of the hooded merganser and common merganser, and very few features in common seem to be present among these three species. The primary male display consists of a rather complex and bizarre series of movements that include a preliminary neck-stretching or "salute" phase and a second neck-dipping or "curtsey" phase, with the entire sequence called the "knicks" (German for "bending"). Males frequently perform the ceremony in synchrony or near-synchrony, and the same display is used as a postcopulatory posture. Pair bonds seem to be rather weak in this species, and some instances of apparent nonmonogamous mating have been observed.

Reproductive Biology. Females begin to search for nest sites as early as two or three weeks before egg-laying begins, and are especially active during early morning hours. Where trees or artificial nest boxes are available the birds will frequently use them, but where such elevated cavities are absent they readily resort to ground-nesting. In Iceland, the majority of the nests are placed in holes or cavities, with shrubs a secondary choice; a few nests are also located under sedge or other herbaceous cover. The birds prefer to nest close to water, and often select island sites if they are available. The average clutch is of nine or ten eggs. Males typically desert their mates early in incubation, which requires an average of about 32 days. Brooding females usually leave their nests only for short periods, and the young birds leave the nest between 12 and 24 hours after hatching. The family may move several miles during their first few days of life, with the young birds sometimes riding on the back of their mother. The fledging period is probably betwen eight and nine weeks, and before the young have fledged they often merge into multi-brood aggregations that sometimes number as many as 100 birds.

Conservation and Status. The breeding-season surveys made by federal biologists do not distinguish red-breasted from common mergansers, but an estimated combined population of nearly 900,000 birds has been suggested by Frank Bellrose, who also calculated that perhaps about 240,000 of these might be red-breasted mergansers. In the absence of better information we must accept this figure, but it would be highly desirable to have more precise data, since most observers believe that the red-breasted merganser has declined on its wintering areas in recent years.

Suggested Reading. Munro and Clemens, 1939.

COMMON MERGANSER (GOOSANDER)
Mergus merganser Linnaeus 1758

Other Vernacular Names: American Goosander, Fish Duck, Sawbill.

Range: Breeds in Iceland, central Europe, Scandinavia, Russia, Siberia to Kamchatka and some of the Bering Sea islands, and in North America from southern Alaska and the southern Yukon eastward across central Canada to James Bay and across the Labrador Peninsula to Newfoundland, southward in the western mountains to California, Arizona, and New Mexico, and northeastward to the Great Lakes, New York, and the New England states. Winters both on salt and fresh water, from the Aleutian Islands to southern California, from Newfoundland to Florida, and in the interior wherever large rivers or deep lakes occur.

North American subspecies:

M. m. americanus Cassin: American Merganser. Breeds in North America as indicated above.

IDENTIFICATION

In the Hand: Immediately recognizable as a merganser on the basis of its long, cylindrical, serrated bill; only the red-breasted merganser has a culmen length as long as this species, from 45 to 60 mm. However, the bill differs in that it (1) has the nostril located in the middle third of the bill, (2) has the feathering on the side of the lower mandible reaching nearly as far forward as that on the side of the upper mandible, (3) has a relatively higher-based and shorter upper mandible that is usually no more than five times as long as high when measured from the mandible edge to the highest unfeathered area, and (4) has a larger, wider nail at its tip. Both sexes are larger than the red-breasted merganser, with adult males and females having minimum folded wing lengths of 280 and 250 mm., respectively.

In the Field: When in nuptial plumage, a male common merganser is unmistakable, with its dark greenish head with a bushy rather than a shaggy crest, its pure white to pinkish breast color, and the absence of gray or black on its sides. Females and immature males appear to have generally grayish to white bodies, strongly contrasting with their reddish brown heads and necks. A clear white throat and a white line between the eye and the base of the bill may be seen under favorable conditions. Sometimes the females utter harsh *karrr* notes, and during aquatic courtship the males produce a rather faint *uig-a* sound reminiscent of the twanging of a guitar string. In flight, a common merganser appears to be a very large, long-necked streamlined duck. It holds its head, neck, and body at the same level; both sexes exhibit a nearly pure white breast color and have almost entirely white underparts, including their underwing surface.

NATURAL HISTORY

Habitat and Foods. The preferred breeding habitat of common mergansers consists of ponds associated with upper portions of rivers in forested regions, and of clear freshwater lakes with forested shorelines. Clear water is needed for visual foraging, and lakes with islands are favored, especially if the islands provide nesting sites in the form of hollow trees or boulder crevices. Because this species is known to be a fish-eater, and often concentrates on rivers having large populations of trout, salmon, and other game species, its foraging behavior and food preferences have been extensively analyzed. Studies in British Columbia and Washington indicate that the birds do consume trout and salmon in areas where these fish are abundant, but they also consume large quantities of sculpins, sticklebacks, and other coarse fish of no economic

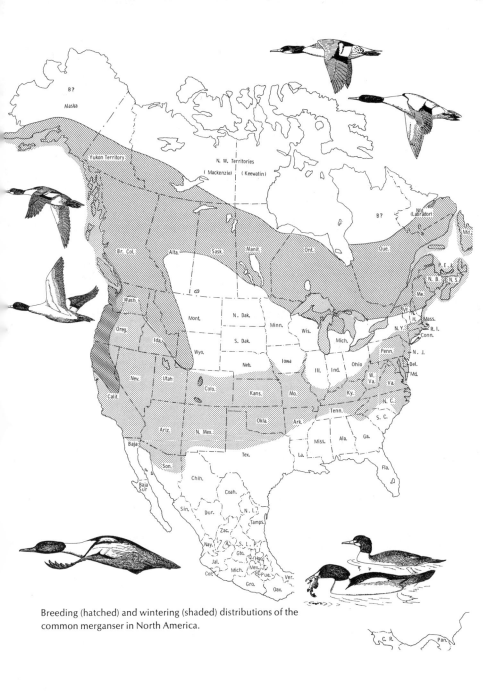

Breeding (hatched) and wintering (shaded) distributions of the common merganser in North America.

importance. Generally the birds concentrate on the more slowly swimming species that can be easily captured, and to this extent the birds are often innocuous and sometimes are even beneficial.

Social Behavior. Common mergansers attain their adult plumages and sexual maturity in their second winter, and during the winter and spring months the birds are frequently occupied in social display. A good deal of chasing is evident during this activity, and females seem to be particularly aggressive toward males that press too close. The males frequently dash over the water surface, sending up a spray of droplets behind them, and sometimes also kick a jet of water backwards with their feet. The most common display is a neck-stretching and fluffing of the head feathers, accompanied by a guitarlike twanging note. A more bell-like call is uttered as the bird suddenly stretches the neck and head vertically in a "salute" posture. Copulation is normally preceded by a mutual drinking display, after which the female becomes prone and the male begins a lengthy series of drinking, preening, shaking, and other postures obviously derived from normal comfort movements.

Reproductive Biology. Females remain rather gregarious during the early stages of the nesting season, while they are searching for suitable nest sites. Where tree cavities are not available the bird will resort to using other well concealed locations, with the primary requirements seeming to be concealment from above and associated darkness in the nest cavity. Besides nesting in natural tree cavities, the birds will also accept nesting boxes. These must be larger than those placed out for wood ducks, with an entrance nearly 5 inches in diameter, and an internal width of about 11 inches. The eggs are laid at a daily rate until a complete clutch of nine or ten eggs is present. Incubation then requires from 32 to 35 days, with the female typically leaving the nest to forage for only a short time each day, usually in the morning hours. After hatching, she usually remains in the nest for a day or two more before leading the young to water. The young are highly precocial and the broods are highly mobile, a situation enhanced by the tendency of the female to carry the youngsters on her back. The fledging period is about 60 to 70 days, but before the young are very old they become quite independent, and increasingly begin to shift for themselves. At about this time the female deserts them to begin her own postnuptial molt, and the juveniles begin to congregate into larger assemblages at favored foraging sites.

Conservation and Status. As noted earlier, reliable information on the population status and trends of all the merganser species is lacking, and we have no good data on the North American population of this large and conspicuous species. One estimate by Frank Bellrose is that there may be about 640,000 birds during the breeding season, but without more specific information nothing can be said about the long-term outlook of this fascinating species.

Suggested Reading. White, 1957.

STIFF-TAILED DUCKS
Tribe Oxyurini

These bizarre diving ducks differ from the rest of the Anatidae in many respects. Of the eight species that are presently recognized, most are placed in the genus *Oxyura*, which name refers to the stiffened, elongated tail feathers typical of the group. In these species the tail feathers extend well beyond the rather short tail coverts and are usually narrow-vaned, so that the individual rectrices tend to separate when spread. The feet are unusually large, and the legs are placed farther to the rear of the body than in any other waterfowl tribe, increasing propulsion efficiency during diving but rendering the birds nearly helpless on land. This grebelike adaptation is paralleled by the evolution of numerous short, glossy body feathers, presumably increasing the effectiveness of waterproofing. In the typical stiff-tails the bill is rather short, broad, and distinctly flattened toward the tip, and virtually all the foraging is done under water. At least in the North American species of stiff-tails, most of the food taken is of vegetable origin. Nests of the typical stiff-tails are built above water, of reed mats or similar vegetation, and often a ramp leads from the nest cup to the water, providing easy access. The birds are quite heavy-bodied and have relatively short wings, so that flight is attained with some difficulty in most species. The masked duck is something of an exception to this point, since its combination of small body size and fairly long wings allows it to land and take off with surprising agility from water of moderate depth.

Only two species of stiff-tails have been reported from North America, and it is most unlikely that any other will occur here by natural means. The ruddy duck is much the more widespread and abundant of these, while the little-known masked duck barely reaches the Mexico–United States border as a breeding species. Indeed, the masked duck is the species most recently added to the list of known breeding North American waterfowl, since it was not until 1967 that firm evidence of its breeding in Texas was established.

MASKED DUCK
Oxyura dominica (Linnaeus) 1766

Other Vernacular Names: None in general use.

Range: Breeds from coastal Texas (rarely), southward through Mexico (probably breeding along the Gulf coast and in the southern interior), Central America, the West Indies, and the lowlands of South America from Colombia to northern Argentina. Probably resident in most areas; winter movements unreported.

Subspecies: None recognized.

IDENTIFICATION

In the Hand: This tiny stiff-tailed duck might be confused only with the ruddy duck, from which it may be distinguished by the white wing speculum, the bill, which is shorter (culmen under 37 mm.) and does not widen appreciably toward the tip, the longer tail (at least 80 mm.), and the large nail, which is not recurved. Unlike the ruddy duck, the outer toe is shorter instead of longer than the middle toe.

In the Field: Although not particularly wary, masked ducks are usually extremely difficult to find in the field, since they usually inhabit marshes extensively overgrown with floating and emergent vegetation, in which the birds mostly remain. The male in nuptial plumage is unmistakable, with its black "mask," long and often cocked tail, and spotted cinnamon color, but most observations in the United States have been of females or femalelike males. These birds are remarkably similar to female ruddy ducks and require considerable care in identification. The white wing markings are never visible unless the bird flies or flaps its wings, both of which are infrequent. The best field mark is the strongly striped facial marking, which consists of three instead of two buffy areas, including a superciliary stripe, an upper cheek stripe, and a buffy cheek and throat area. Female ruddy ducks have only two buffy areas and completely lack any pale stripe above the eye. When the birds take off they rarely fly high, but usually skim the marsh vegetation, suddenly slowing and dropping vertically downward out of sight of the marsh. Both sexes are normally quiet, although some calls have been attributed to the male.

NATURAL HISTORY

Habitat and Foods. The breeding habitat of this species consists of tropical-like marshes or swamps, densely vegetated with emergent plant life and usually having lily pads, water hyacinths, or other floating-leaf aquatic plants extensively covering the water surface. Most breeding records are from freshwater habitats, but the birds are sometimes also seen in mangrove swamps. Probably little or no migration is typical over the species' major range, and thus nonbreeding habitats are apparently the same as those used during the breeding season. Rather little is known about the foods and foraging of masked ducks. The few specimens that have been examined as to foods they consumed contained seeds of various aquatic and terrestrial plants. The birds apparently forage by diving, and usually are found in ponds that are not very deep. Although the ponds usually have water lilies on them as well, it is not known whether the seeds of this plant are an important source of food or whether its leaves simply provide effective visual protection from possible aerial predators.

Social Behavior. Unfortunately, almost nothing is known with certainty about the social behavior of this interesting species. The age of sexual maturity is not known but presumably is a year, and the birds are also apparently monogamous, with temporary pair bonds. Very little pair-forming behavior has been seen in wild birds, however, and neither the time of pair formation nor the associated display behavior has been documented. All other stiff-tailed ducks are known to have

Breeding distribution of the masked duck in North and Central America. Extralimital (non-Texas) U.S. records since 1950 are also indicated.

●=Extralimital Specimen Records
○=Extralimital Sight Records

rather elaborate displays involving an inflation of the neck region and cocking of the elongated tail. Both of these elements have been described for the masked duck, but beyond this, little is certain. Some rather loud calls as well as nearly inaudible ones have been attributed to the male, and females are said to produce hissing sounds. No information is available on copulatory behavior.

Reproductive Biology. Very few nests of masked ducks have been found, and not much is known of their nesting behavior. In South America the birds have been reported to be fall breeders, with nesting occurring during the time that water levels were rising in rice fields. The nest is said to be placed in rushes, or in a deep cup in rice stems, just above the water level. Normally, they are beside deep water into which the female can readily escape, and they frequently have a lateral entry and a roofed-over top. The clutch size is generally believed to be about four to six eggs, but at least in some areas averages nearly twice that number, perhaps as a result of dump-nesting or parasitic behavior. The probable egg-laying rate is one egg per day, and the incubation period is believed to be about 28 days. Incubation is evidently done entirely by the female, as no males have been seen in the vicinity of nests or broods. After the eggs have hatched the young are apparently often brought back to the nest at night for roosting. The fledging period is unknown, but one closely observed brood disappeared after about 45 days, presumably having fledged.

Conservation and Status. To a greater degree than any of the other known breeding species of North American waterfowl, the masked duck must be considered a marginal species. It is only known to have nested a few times within the United States, and the first definite record of breeding here occurred as recently as 1967. This bird is highly secretive and inconspicuous, and little can be done to help insure its continuation as a breeding species within the limits of the United States.

Suggested Reading. Johnsgard and Hagemeyer, 1969.

RUDDY DUCK
Oxyura jamaicensis (Gmelin) 1789

Other Vernacular Names: Butterball, Stiff-tail.

Range: Breeds from central British Columbia to southwestern Mackenzie District, across the Canadian prairies to the Red River valley of Manitoba, with sporadic breedings in southern Ontario and Quebec, and southward through the western and central United States to Baja California, coastal Texas, and occasionally eastward to the Great Lakes or beyond. Also breeds in the West Indies, the Central Valley of Mexico, and in various Andean lakes from Colombia to Chile. Winters in North America from British Columbia along the coast and to a limited extent inland through the western United States and south to Mexico and Central America, along the Atlantic coast from Massachusetts to Florida, in the West Indies, and along the Gulf coast.

North American subspecies:

O. *j. jamaicensis* (Gmelin): North American Ruddy Duck. Breeds in North America as indicated above. Regarded by the A.O.U. (1957) as O.*j. rubida* (Wilson).

IDENTIFICATION

In the Hand: Excepting the very rare masked duck, ruddy ducks can be easily distinguished from all other North American ducks by their long, narrow tail feathers and their short, wide, flattened bill. Ruddy ducks are the only North American species in which the nail of the bill is narrow and small on the upper mandible surface but wide and recurved below the tip. Ruddy ducks also differ from masked ducks in that they lack any white on the wings, the outer toe is as long or longer than the middle toe, and the bills are longer (culmen length 37 to 44 mm.).

In the Field: Except during fairly late spring and summer, ruddy ducks of both sexes are in a rather brownish and inconspicuous plumage. On the water they appear as very chunky diving ducks, with short necks and a long tail either held on the water surface or variably cocked above it. The whitish cheeks, which are streaked with brown in females, are the most conspicuous field marks at this time, but as spring progresses the male assumes an increasingly bluish bill and a more reddish body plumage, together with a contrasting black crown. Ruddy ducks seem to have greater difficulty in taking flight than any other North American duck, including the masked duck. They patter along the water for some distance before attaining their characteristic buzzing flight, with their short wings beating furiously to keep the bird aloft. Neither sex is highly vocal, but the female utters a rare squeaky threat call, and during display males produce a dull thumping noise that terminates in a weak croak.

NATURAL HISTORY

Habitat and Foods. The breeding habitat of ruddy ducks consists of permanent or alkaline marshes having emergent vegetation and relatively stable water levels. Suitable nesting habitat must also have open water in fairly close proximity to nesting cover, including emergent plants that provide accessibility as well as adequate cover density, and additionally can be bent down by the birds. Water passageways such as muskrat channels that permit easy movement between the nest site and open water are also needed. The foods of ruddy ducks contain a high proportion of plant materials, including stems, leaves, seeds, and tubers

Breeding (hatched) and wintering (shaded) distributions of the ruddy duck in North America.

of aquatic plants. There is also a high incidence of insect consumption, especially during summer, and during the winter mollusks and crustaceans probably increase in significance, especially in brackish-water habitats. The birds forage primarily by diving, and their flattened bill seems to be well adapted for probing in muddy bottoms and sifting out small particles or organisms.

Social Behavior. Ruddy ducks acquire their nuptial plumages in the first year of life, with males not coming into full breeding plumage until rather late in the spring. Social display thus usually begins rather late, and continues well into the breeding season. Males seem to confine most of their display to the areas in which they are actually breeding, and thus display seems to serve as much for territorial proclamation as it does for pair-bond formation or maintenance. Although some species of stiff-tails are known to be entirely promiscuous and their displays are directed toward territoriality and attraction of females for mating, this species seems to form at least transient pair bonds. However, the common belief that males remain attached to their mates through the incubation period and help in rearing the young is a result of misinterpretation of observation of males trying to associate with females leading young. At that time, as indeed during the prenesting period, the usual response of the female is an aggressive gaping or threatening jab toward the male.

Reproductive Biology. Females typically build their nests in heavy emergent cover, with hardstem bulrush being a favorite. Other bulrushes and cattails are also used, although the relative ease with which the plant can be bent over and formed into a nest seems to be an important aspect in choosing nest cover. Additionally the water depth of the nest site is important, with a depth of about a foot seemingly being favored. Nests often have ramps leading up to the cup, and additionally are usually provided with a convenient escape route to deep water. The average clutch is of about eight eggs, which are laid at the rate of about one per day. However, clutch sizes are frequently inflated by parasitically laid eggs or dump-nesting by several females. Incubation requires 23 to 26 days, and frequently at the time of hatching of most of the clutch one or more only partially incubated eggs will remain in the nest, probably the result of parasitism late in the incubation period. The fledging period is probably between 52 and 66 days, but the young are highly precocial and rarely does the brood remain intact for this entire period.

Conservation and Status. This is one of the most entrancing of all North American waterfowl, and unfortunately is also one of the most susceptible of all species to habitat disruption. Its dependence on prairie marshes and stable water levels during the time of nesting makes it highly vulnerable to nest destruction from flooding or drought, and even under the best of conditions its nesting success seems to be rather low. Breeding-season surveys suggest that the average North American population of ruddy ducks may be about 475,000 birds, but there have been enormous year-to-year variations in these figures.

Suggested Reading. Low, 1941; Joyner, 1975.

Identification Key to
North American Waterfowl

The key on the following pages provides an efficient means of identifying virtually all North American waterfowl that may be examined in the hand. The procedure for using it is comparable to that used for all such dual-choice or "dichotomous" keys. One simply chooses which of the initial descriptive couplets (A or A′) best fits the unknown bird. Having chosen one of these, the pair of descriptive couplets (a and a′) immediately below the chosen alternative is next considered, without further regard for the rejected one. Subsequent choices, which are sequentially numbered (1 and 1′, 2 and 2′, etc.) must then be considered until the name of the species has been reached. In no case will more than eleven choices be required to identify any of the 50 waterfowl species or subspecies represented in the key. After having tentatively determined the identity of the unknown bird, one should refer to the appropriate "Identification" sections of the text, to confirm or reject the initial determination. Illustrations in this book or other references should also be consulted, bearing in mind that sexual or seasonal variations in plumage may exist.

A. Legs with completely reticulated (networklike) scale pattern, iridescent colors absent from plumage (geese, swans, and whistling ducks)

  a. Smaller (folded wing under 300 mm.*), legs extended beyond the tail (whistling ducks)

    1. Bill blackish, upper wing surface lacking white patterning . . . **Fulvous Whistling Duck**

    1′ Bill red in adults, extensively white on upper wing surface . . . **Black-bellied Whistling Duck**

  a′. Larger (folded wing over 300 mm.), legs not extending beyond the tail

---

*Wing lengths are of folded, unflattened wings; culmen length is measured from tip of bill to edge of forehead feathers.

1. Primaries white (swans)
  2. Bill usually reddish, with variably large black knob at base, longest primaries more than 7 cm. longer than the outer ones . . . **Mute Swan**
  2'. Bill usually black (flesh-colored in juveniles), longest primaries not more than 7 cm. longer than outer ones, bill never with knob at base
    3. Bill usually with yellow present in front of eyes, weight under 20 pounds, folded wing under 575 mm., less than 50 mm. from tip of bill to anterior end of nostril . . . **Whistling Swan**
    3' Bill usually without any yellow in front of eyes, weight often over 20 pounds, folded wing at least 540 mm. in adults, usually at least 50 mm. from tip of bill to anterior end of nostril . . . **Trumpeter Swan**
1'. Primaries not white (geese)
  2. Legs, feet, and bill black, head and neck plumage mostly black
    3. White present on cheeks
      4. White cheeks extending above eyes and across forehead, breast black . . . **Barnacle Goose** (casual visitor)
      4'. White cheeks not extending in front of eyes, breast brown . . . **Canada Goose**
    3'. White absent from cheeks . . . **Brant Goose**
  2'. Legs, feet, and bill variously reddish, yellow, or flesh-colored, never black
    3. Under tail coverts white, throat brown or white
      4. Feet orange to yellow, white on head lacking or limited to narrow area in front of eyes . . . **White-fronted Goose**
      4'. Feet red, pink, or flesh-colored, head often entirely white
        5. Smaller (folded wing under 400 mm.), bill short and often warty at base, lacking definite black "grinning patch" . . . **Ross Goose**
        5'. Larger (wing over 400 mm.), bill longer and never warty at base, with definite black "grinning patch" at sides . . . **Snow (and "Blue") Goose**
    3'. Under tail coverts gray, throat black . . . **Emperor Goose**

A′. Legs with lower part of tarsus having scutellate (vertically aligned) scales, iridescent coloration often present on wings or body (typical ducks)

   a. Feet with weakly lobed hind toe, middle toe longer than outer toe, iridescent color usually present on wing surface (perching and dabbling ducks)

      1. Upper wing surface mostly iridescent bluish or purplish, tail long and rather square-tipped, claws relatively sharp . . . **Wood Duck**

     1′. Upper wing surface not iridescent except on secondary feathers, tail usually short and rounded (sometimes pointed), claws not especially sharp (dabbling ducks)

        2. Middle and lesser upper wing coverts white, pale gray, or light blue

           3. Feet gray, upper wing coverts gray or white

              4. Tertials greatly elongated and sickle-shaped, underwing lining white, head crested . . . **Falcated Duck** (accidental visitor)

             4′. Tertials not greatly elongated or sickle-shaped, underwing lining gray, head uncrested

                5. Axillar feathers mottled with dark gray . . . **European Wigeon** (casual visitor)

               5′. Axillar feathers white or only slightly flecked with gray . . . **American Wigeon**

          3′. Feet yellow or orange, upper wing coverts bluish

             4. Bill spatulate (spoon-shaped) . . . **Shoveler**

            4′. Bill normally shaped or only slightly spatulate

               5. Bill uniformly narrow for most of its length (maximum 44 mm.), rusty cinnamon color absent, head with white crescent (males) or brownish with clear buffy to white spot between eye and bill . . . **Blue-winged Teal**

              5′. Bill longer (minimum 41 mm.) and slightly spatulate toward tip, rusty cinnamon or yellowish color often present on body, head uniformly cinnamon (males) or brownish with darker streaking that usually obscures the pale area between the eye and bill . . . **Cinnamon Teal**

     2′. Middle and lesser upper wing coverts grayish brown or brown

3. Wing speculum iridescent blue, violet, or bluish green, with black (or black and white) bars in front and behind; feet yellow to reddish

   4. White present both in front of and behind the speculum

      5. Vermiculations present on tertials (males), or the tertials grayish (females); females with white or nearly white under tail coverts and white on most or all rectrices . . . **Common Mallard**

      5'. Vermiculations never present on tertials, the tertials brownish with green cast; under tail coverts dark brown with lighter edging; white, if present on rectrices, limited to three outer feathers . . . **Mexican Mallard**

   4'. White present only behind the speculum, or altogether absent from upper wing surface

      5. Tawny coloration present in front of black bar on greater secondary coverts, predominant body color tawny brown . . . **Florida and Mottled Mallards**

      5'. Tawny coloration absent from secondary coverts, predominant body color dark brown . . . **Black Duck**

3'. Wing speculum not as described above, legs and feet usually grayish

   4. Speculum iridescent green and black, lined in front with cinnamon buff or buffy white

      5. Folded wing over 220 mm., buffy white present in front of speculum, which is green on outer secondaries . . . **Falcated Duck** (accidental visitor)

      5'. Folded wing under 220 mm., cinnamon-tinted in front of speculum, which is black on outer secondaries

         6. Middle tail feathers over 75 mm., black outer secondaries widely tipped with white . . . **Baikal Teal** (accidental visitor)

         6'. Middle tail feathers under 75 mm., black outer secondaries only narrowly tipped with white . . . **Green-winged Teal**

   4'. Speculum not green and black; if green is present at all it is limited to the anterior half of the speculum

      5. Secondaries white, gray, and black, with black extend-

ing to the secondary coverts, tail rounded, underwing lining white . . . **Gadwall**

5′. Secondaries lacking black, or black is limited to a narrow bar at rear of speculum; tail variably pointed; underwing lining dusky or brownish

6. Speculum iridescent green anteriorly, throat and cheeks white, bill reddish at base . . . **Bahama Pintail** (accidental visitor)

6′. Speculum bronze to copper-colored, or lacking iridescence and brownish; cheeks never white and bill never with reddish color . . . **Pintail**

a′. Feet with strongly lobed hind toe, iridescent coloration usually lacking on wings (two exceptions), length of outer toe usually greater than that of middle toe (one exception), body generally adapted for diving (pochards, sea ducks, and stiff-tailed ducks)

1. Bill narrow, cylindrical, serrated at the edges and with a hooked tip (mergansers)

2. Smaller (folded wing under 200 mm.), bill short and gray to black, feet gray or yellowish

3. Upper forewing and tertials white, no definite crest . . . **Smew** (accidental visitor)

3′. Upper forewing brown or mottled grayish white, head crested . . . **Hooded Merganser**

2′. Larger (folded wing over 200 mm.), bill long and reddish, feet orange to red

3. Nostril nearer to base of bill than center, feathering at base of upper mandible extending farther forward than that of lower mandible . . . **Red-breasted Merganser**

3′. Nostril nearer to middle of bill than base, feathering at base of upper and lower mandible extending about equal distance forward . . . **Common Merganser**

1′. Bill not as described above

2. Tail feathers unusually long and narrow, bill broad and flattened at tip, wings relatively short, and legs placed well to the rear of the body (stiff-tailed ducks)

3. White present on secondaries, nail of bill not recurved, outer toe not longer than middle toe . . . **Masked Duck**

3′. White lacking on wings, nail of bill recurved, outer toe longer than middle toe . . . **Ruddy Duck**

2′. Tail feathers not unusually long and narrow; bill variously shaped; wings not unusually short, and legs only moderately situated toward rear of body (pochards and typical sea ducks)

3. Secondaries with iridescent bluish speculum, tail somewhat pointed

    4. Inner secondaries curved outwardly, underwing surface white . . . **Steller Eider**

    4′. Inner secondaries not curved, underwing surface dusky . . . **Harlequin Duck**

3′. No iridescence on wing, the secondaries brown, gray, or white, tail either rounded or pointed

    4. Very small (folded wing under 190 mm.), white present behind eye . . . **Bufflehead**

    4′. Larger (folded wing over 200 mm.), white present or absent on head

        5. Feathering present along sides or top of bill almost to nostrils or sometimes beyond

        6. Tertials straight and little or no longer than secondaries

        7. Feathering on sides of bill, white present on secondaries . . . **White-winged Scoter**

        7′. Feathering present on top of bill, no white present on secondaries . . . **Surf Scoter**

        6′. Tertials elongated and curved outwardly

        7. Feathering on bill extending farther on sides than on top, extending laterally to a point below the nostrils . . . **Common Eider**

        7′. Feathering on top of bill extending farther than on sides, never with feathering below the nostrils

        8. Top of nostrils almost hidden by feathers, pale buffy or white area around eyes . . . **Spectacled Eider**

        8′. No feathering near nostrils, unfeathered basal enlargement of bill almost reaches the eyes . . . **King Eider**

5'. No feathering present on top or sides of bill

  6. White markings present on upper wing surface

    7. White largely limited to the secondaries (sometimes extending to inner primaries); upper wing coverts gray, brown, or black; feet gray

      8. Back blackish or dusky brown, bill only slightly wider (up to 4 mm.) near tip than at base, with long or rudimentary crest present . . . **Tufted Duck** (accidental visitor)

      8'. Back grayish white or dusky brown, bill definitely wider (at least 5 mm.) near tip than at base, never distinctly crested

        9. White of wings extending to inner primaries, nail of bill at least 8 mm. wide . . . **Greater Scaup**

        9'. White of wings limited to secondaries (inner primaries may be quite pale), nail of bill under 7 mm. wide . . . **Lesser Scaup**

    7'. White or pale gray markings present on upper wing coverts, tertials, or both, feet yellow to orange

      8. Bill gradually tapering in width from base, nail of bill raised and at least 12 mm. long . . . **Barrow Goldeneye**

      8'. Bill about as wide at nostrils as at base, nail of bill relatively flattened and no more than 11 mm. long . . . **Common Goldeneye**

  6'. No white markings on upper wing surface

    7. Secondaries gray to grayish white, at least more grayish or paler than primaries, tail rounded and no more than 75 mm. long

      8. Bill with one (females) or two (males) pale rings, folded wing under 210 mm., upper forewing and back dark brown or black . . . **Ring-necked Duck**

      8'. Bill with only one pale ring or none, folded wing at least 210 mm., forewing and back gray or light brown

        9. Bill long (exposed culmen over 50 mm.), and forehead sloping; upper wing coverts with vermiculations . . . **Canvasback**

9'. Bill shorter (exposed culmen under 50 mm.), and with a high forehead; upper wing coverts not vermiculated . . . **Redhead**

7'. Secondaries brown or blackish, no lighter than rest of wing; tail slightly or greatly pointed and usually longer than 75 mm. centrally

8. White or pale gray feathers present on flanks, a variable amount of white (sometimes only a narrow ring) around eye . . . **Oldsquaw**

8'. Flanks brown, reddish brown, or black; white lacking around eye or limited to areas below and in front of eye

9. Outer (10th) primaries narrower and shorter than adjacent ones, bill fairly long (over 40 mm.) and somewhat enlarged basally . . . **Black Scoter**

9'. Outer primaries not narrow and shorter than adjacent ones, bill short (under 30 mm.) and not enlarged basally . . . **Harlequin Duck**

Key for Head Profiles
of North American Waterfowl

Plate 1. Swans, geese, and whistling ducks

1. Fulvous whistling duck, adult
2. Black-bellied whistling duck, adult
3. Mute swan, adult
4. Trumpeter swan, adult
5. Whistling swan, adult
6. White-fronted goose, adult
7. Snow goose (blue phase), adult
8. Ross goose, adult
9. Emperor goose, adult
10. Canada goose, adult
11. Brant goose, adult
12. Barnacle goose, adult

Plate 2. Male surface-feeding and perching ducks

13. Wood duck
14. American wigeon
15. European wigeon
16. Falcated duck
17. Gadwall
18. Baikal teal
19. Green-winged teal
20. Common mallard
21. Black duck
22. Bahama pintail
23. Pintail
24. Garganey
25. Blue-winged teal
26. Cinnamon teal
27. Northern shoveler

Plate 3. Female surface-feeding and perching ducks

28. Wood duck
29. American wigeon
30. European wigeon
31. Falcated duck
32. Gadwall
33. Baikal teal
34. Green-winged teal
35. Common mallard
36. Black duck
37. Florida mallard
38. Pintail
39. Garganey
40. Blue-winged teal
41. Cinnamon teal
42. Northern shoveler

Plate 4. Male pochards and typical sea ducks

43. Canvasback
44. Redhead
45. Ring-necked duck
46. Tufted duck
47. Greater scaup
48. Lesser scaup
49. King eider
50. Common eider

51. Spectacled eider
52. Steller eider
53. Harlequin duck
54. Oldsquaw
55. Black scoter
56. Surf scoter
57. White-winged scoter

Plate 5. Female pochards and typical sea ducks

58. Canvasback
59. Redhead
60. Ring-necked duck
61. Tufted duck
62. Greater scaup
63. Lesser scaup
64. Common eider
65. King eider

66. Spectacled eider
67. Steller eider
68. Harlequin duck
69. Oldsquaw
70. Black scoter
71. Surf scoter
72. White-winged scoter

Plate 6. Goldeneyes, mergansers, and stiff-tails

73. Bufflehead, male
74. Bufflehead, female
75. Common goldeneye, male
76. Common goldeneye, female
77. Barrow goldeneye, male
78. Barrow goldeneye, female
79. Smew, male
80. Smew, female
81. Hooded merganser, male

82. Hooded merganser, female
83. Common merganser, male
84. Common merganser, female
85. Red-breasted merganser, male
86. Red-breasted merganser, female
87. Masked duck, male
88. Masked duck, female
89. Ruddy duck, male
90. Ruddy duck, female

References

Aldrich, J. W. (1946). "Speciation in the white-cheeked geese." *Wilson Bulletin,* 58:94-103.

Aldrich, J. W., and K. P. Baer. (1970). "Status and speciation in the Mexican duck *(Anas diazi)*." *Wilson Bulletin,* 82:63-73.

Alison, R. M. (1975). "Breeding biology and behavior of the oldsquaw *(Clangula hyemalis* L.)." *Ornithological Monographs,* No. 18. 52 pp.

American Ornithologists' Union. (1957). *Check-list of North American Birds.* 5th ed. Baltimore: Lord Baltimore Press, Inc.

Banko, W. E. (1960). "The trumpeter swan: Its history, habits, and population in the United States." U. S. Dept. of Interior, Fish and Wildlife Service, North American Fauna, No. 63. pp. 1-214.

Banks, R. G. (1978). "Nomenclature of the black-bellied whistling duck." *Auk,* 95:348-352.

Barry, T. W. (1966). "Geese of the Anderson River delta, Northwest Territories, Canada." Ph.D. dissertation, University of Alberta, Edmonton.

Bellrose, F. C. (1976). *Ducks, geese and swans of North America.* Harrisburg: Stackpole Books.

Bengtson, S. (1966). "Field studies on the harlequin duck in Iceland." *Wildfowl Trust Annual Report,* 17:79-94.

——. (1972). "Breeding ecology of the harlequin *Histrionicus histrionicus* (L.) in Iceland." *Ornis Scandinavica,* 3:25-43.

Bent, A. C. (1925). "Life histories of North American wild fowl." Part 2. U. S. National Museum Bulletin, 130:1-316.

Bolen, E. G., B. McDaniel, and C. Cottam. (1964). "Natural history of the black-bellied tree duck *(Dendrocygna autumnalis)* in southern Texas." *Southwestern Naturalist,* 9:78-88.

Brandt, H. (1943). *Alaska bird trails.* Cleveland: Bird Research Foundation.

Brooks, A. (1920). "Notes on some American ducks." *Auk,* 37:353-367.

Byrd, G. V., D. L. Johnson, and D. D. Gibson. (1974). "The birds of Adak Island, Alaska." *Condor,* 76:288-300.

Carter, B. C. (1958). "The American goldeneye in central New Brunswick." Canadian Wildlife Service, Wildlife Management Bulletin, Series 2, No. 9. 47 pp.

Cooch, F. G. (1965). "The breeding biology and management of the northern eider (*Somateria mollissima borealis*) in the Cape Dorset area, Northwest Territories." Canadian Wildlife Service, Wildlife Management Bulletin, Series 2, No. 10. 68 pp.

Coulter, M. W., and W. R. Miller. (1968). "Nesting biology of black ducks and mallards in northern New England." Vermont Fish and Game Department Bulletin, No. 68-2. 74 pp.

Dane, C. W. (1966). "Some aspects of the breeding biology of the blue-winged teal." *Auk*, 83:389-402.

Dau, C. P. (1974). "Nesting biology of the spectacled eider *Somateria fischeri* (Brandt) on the Yukon-Kuskokwim Delta, Alaska." M.S. thesis, University of Alaska, Fairbanks. 72 pp.

Delacour, J. (1954–1964). *The waterfowl of the world*. 4 vols. London: Country Life.

Delacour, J., and S. D. Ripley. (1975). "Description of a new subspecies of the white-fronted goose *Anser albifrons*." *American Museum Novitates*, 2565:1-4.

Dickinson, J. C., Jr. (1953). "Report on the McCabe collection of British Columbian birds." Harvard University, Museum of Comparative Zoology, Bulletin, 109:121-209.

Eisenhauer, D. I., and C. M. Kirkpatrick. (1977). "Ecology of the emperor goose in Alaska." *Wildlife Monographs*, No. 57. 62 pp.

Elgas, R. (1970). "Breeding populations of tule white-fronted geese in northwestern Canada." *Wilson Bulletin*, 82:420-426.

Erskine, A. J. (1972). *Buffleheads*. Canadian Wildlife Service Monograph Series, No. 4. Ottawa: Information Canada.

Gates, J. M. (1962). "Breeding biology of the gadwall in northern Utah." *Wilson Bulletin*, 74:43-67.

Gerhman, K. H. (1951). "An ecological study of the lesser scaup duck (*Aythya affinis* Eyton) at West Medical Lake, Spokane County, Washington." M.S. thesis, Washington State University, Pullman.

Grice, D., and J. P. Rogers. (1965). "The wood duck in Massachusetts." Massachusetts Division of Fisheries and Game, Final Report, Proj. No. W-19-R. 196 pp.

Hansen, H. A., P. E. K. Shepherd, J. G. King, and W. A. Troyer. (1971). "The trumpeter swan in Alaska." *Wildlife Monographs*, No. 26. 83 pp.

Hanson, H. C. (1965). *The giant Canada goose*. Carbondale: Southern Illinois University Press.

Hochbaum, H. A. (1943). *The canvasback on a prairie marsh*. Washington, D. C.: Wildlife Management Institute, and Harrisburg: Stackpole Co.

Hubbard, J. P. (1977). "The biological and taxonomic status of the Mexican duck." New Mexico Department of Fish and Game, Bulletin No. 16. 56 pp.

Huey, W. S. (1961). "Comparison of female mallard with female Mexican duck." *Auk*, 78:428-431.

Johnsgard, P. A. (1961). "Evolutionary relationships among the North American mallards." *Auk*, 78:1-43.

_____. (1965) *Handbook of waterfowl behavior*. Ithaca: Cornell University Press.

_____. (1974). *Song of the north wind: A story of the snow goose*. New York: Doubleday.

_____. (1975). *Waterfowl of North America*. Bloomington: Indiana University Press.

_____. (1978). *Ducks, geese and swans of the world*. Lincoln: University of Nebraska Press.

Johnsgard, P. A., and D. Hagemeyer. (1969). "The masked duck in the United States." *Auk*, 84:691-695.

Joyner, D. W. (1975). "Nest parasitism and brood-related behavior of the ruddy duck (*Oxyura jamaicensis rubida*)." Ph.D. dissertation, University of Nebraska, Lincoln.

Keith, L. B. (1961). "A study of waterfowl ecology on small impoundments in southeastern Alberta." *Wildlife Monographs*, No. 6. 88 pp.

Kistchinski, A. A., and V. E. Flint. (1974). "On the biology of the spectacled eider." *Wildfowl*, 25:5-15.

Koskimies, J., and E. Routamo. (1953). "Zur Fortpflanzungsbiologie der Samtente *Melanitta f. fusca* (L.). 1. Allgemeine Nistokologie." Papers on Game Research (*Riistatietelliaia Julkaisuja*), 10:1-105.

Kuchel, C. R. (1977). Some aspects of the behavior and ecology of harlequin ducks breeding in Glacier National Park, Montana. M.S. thesis, University of Montana, Missoula.

Leopold, A. S. (1959). *Wildlife of Mexico: The game birds and mammals*. Berkeley: University of California Press.

Low, J. B. (1941). "Nesting of the ruddy duck in Iowa." *Auk*, 58:506-517.

MacInnes, C. D. (1966). "Population behavior of Eastern Arctic Canada geese. *Journal of Wildlife Management*, 30:536-553.

Manning, T. H., E. O. Höhn, and A. H. Macpherson. (1956). "The birds of Banks Island." National Museums of Canada Bulletin No. 143:1-144.

McCartney, R. B. (1963). "The fulvous tree duck in Louisiana." M.S. thesis, Louisiana State University, Baton Rouge.

McKinney, F. (1965). "The displays of the American green-winged teal." *Wilson Bulletin*, 77:112-121.

————. (1967). "Breeding behavior of captive shovelers." *Wildfowl Trust Annual Report*, 18:108-121.

————. (1970). "Displays of four species of blue-winged ducks." *Living Bird*, 9:29-64.

Meanley, B., and A. G. Meanley. (1959). "Observations on the fulvous tree duck in Louisiana." *Wilson Bulletin*, 71:33-45.

Mendall, H. L. (1958). "The ring-necked duck in the Northeast." *University of Maine Bulletin*, 60(16), and *University of Maine Studies*, Second Series, No. 73:1-317.

Mickelson, P. G. (1975). "Breeding biology of cackling geese (*Branta canadensis minima* Ridgway) and associated species on the Yukon-Kuskokwim Delta, Alaska." *Wildlife Monographs*, No. 45. 35 pp.

Morse, T. E., J. L. Jakabosky, and V. P. McCrow. (1969). "Some aspects of the breeding biology of the hooded merganser." *Journal of Wildlife Management*, 30:596-604.

Munro, J. A. (1939). "Studies of waterfowl on British Columbia. Barrow's golden-eye, American golden-eye." *Transactions Royal Canadian Institute*, 22:259-318.

Munro, J. A., and W. A. Clemens. (1939). "The food and feeding habits of the red-breasted merganser in British Columbia." *Journal of Wildlife Management*, 3:46-53.

Oring, L. W. (1969). "Summer biology of the gadwall at Delta, Manitoba." *Wilson Bulletin*, 81:44-54.

Parmelee, D. F., H. A. Stephens, and R. H. Schmidt. (1967). "The birds of southeastern Victoria Island and adjacent small islands." *National Museums of Canada Bulletin*, 222:1-229.

Rogers, J. P. (1964). "Effect of drought on reproduction of the lesser scaup." *Journal of Wildlife Management*, 28:213-222.

Ryder, J. P. (1967). "The breeding biology of Ross' goose in the Perry

River region, Northwest Territories." Canadian Wildlife Service Report Series, No. 3, pp. 1-56.

Scott, P., and the Wildfowl Trust. (1972). *The swans.* London: Michael Joseph.

Sowls, L. K. (1978). *Prairie ducks: A study of their behavior, ecology, and management.* Lincoln: University of Nebraska Press.

Spencer, H. E., Jr. (1953). "The cinnamon teal (*Anas cyanoptera* Vieillot): Its life history, ecology, and management." M.S. thesis, Utah State University, Logan.

Todd, W. E. C. (1963). *Birds of the Labrador Peninsula and adjacent areas.* Toronto: University of Toronto Press.

Trauger, D., A. Dzubin, and J. P. Ryder. (1971). "White geese intermediate between Ross' geese and lesser snow geese." *Auk*, 88:856-875.

Weller, M. W. (1959). "Parasitic egg laying in the redhead (*Aythya americana*) and other North American Anatidae." *Ecological Monographs*, 29:333-365.

Weller, M. W., D. L. Trauger, and G. L. Krapu. (1969). "Breeding birds of the West Mirage Islands, Great Slave Lake, N.W.T." *Canadian Field-Naturalist*, 83:344-360.

White, H. C. (1957). "Food and natural history of mergansers on salmon waters in the Maritime Provinces of Canada." Fisheries Research Board of Canada Bulletin, 116:1-63.

Willey, C. H., and B. F. Halla. (1972). "Mute swans of Rhode Island." Rhode Island Department of Natural Resources, Wildlife Pamphlet No. 8. 47 pp.

Williams, C. S. (1967). *Honker: A discussion of the habits and needs of the largest of our Canada geese.* Princeton: D. Van Nostrand Co.

Williamson, F. S. L., M. C. Thompson, and J. Q. Hines. (1966). "Avifaunal investigations." In U.S. Atomic Energy Commission, *Environment of the Cape Thompson Region, Alaska*, pp. 437-480.

Wright, B. S. (1954). *High tide and an east wind: The story of the black duck.* Washington, D. C.: Wildlife Management Institute and Harrisburg: Stackpole Co.

Index

English vernacular names of waterfowl indexed here are in general those used in this book for species or larger groupings. Vernacular names for sub-species are only indexed to those pages where they may be listed among the subspecies included in the species accounts. Pages that include the primary discussions of each species are indicated by boldface under the species' vernacular name and its scientific name. Species other than waterfowl are not indexed.